Learning from Libraries That Use

WordPress

Learning from Libraries That Use
WordPress

Content-Management System
Best Practices and Case Studies

Kyle M. L. Jones / Polly-Alida Farrington

AMERICAN LIBRARY ASSOCIATION | CHICAGO 2013

Kyle M. L. Jones is a PhD student at the University of Wisconsin–Madison in the School of Library and Information Studies, where his research interests include e-learning informatics, traditional and nontraditional online learning environments, and digital library technologies. He received his BA in English literature and secondary education from Elmhurst College in Elmhurst, Illinois, and his MLIS from Dominican University in River Forest, Illinois.

Polly-Alida Farrington is a consultant and the owner of PA Farrington Associates, with more than fifteen years' experience providing technology-related training, web project development, and consulting services to libraries, library systems, and schools. A former academic librarian, she has seventeen years' experience in reference, government documents, interlibrary loan, and technology. Her website is www.pafa.net.

Printed in the United States of America
17 16 15 14 13   5 4 3 2 1

Extensive effort has gone into ensuring the reliability of the information in this book; however, the publisher makes no warranty, express or implied, with respect to the material contained herein.

ISBNs: 978-0-8389-1162-4 (paper); 978-0-8389-9610-2 (PDF). For more information on digital formats, visit the ALA Store at alastore.ala.org and select eEditions.

Library of Congress Cataloging-in-Publication Data
Jones, Kyle M. L.
 Learning from libraries that use WordPress : content-management system best practices and case studies / Kyle M.L. Jones and Polly-Alida Farrington.
     pages   cm
 Includes bibliographical references and index.
 ISBN 978-0-8389-1162-4
 1. Library Web sites—Design. 2. WordPress (Electronic resource) 3. Blogs—Computer programs. 4. Web sites—Authoring programs. 5. Library Web sites—Case studies. I. Farrington, Polly-Alida. II. Title.
 Z674.75.W67J66 2013
 025.042'2—dc23
                                                                                    2012010063

Book design in ITC Esprit Std, Byington, and Bell Gothic Std by Casey Bayer.
Cover image © knikola/Shutterstock, Inc.

♾ This paper meets the requirements of ANSI/NISO Z39.48-1992 (Permanence of Paper).

Contents

Foreword

In recent years libraries of all types and all sizes have been engaging in online content creation. And who better to partake in such an activity than the intellectual centers of communities, campuses, and organizations? With the breadth of material at hand and knowledge workers—librarians—willing, there's a lot to share. Stable publishing platforms have emerged for diverse needs. We have services like Twitter and Facebook for social networking; we have tools like Blogger and WordPress.com for blogging; and we turn to open source content-management systems such as Drupal for our library websites. Our online publishing needs, and the tools and services used to fulfill those needs, are disparate.

In this book, authors Kyle M. L. Jones and Polly-Alida Farrington introduce an excellent addition to our technology toolbox that might just surprise you with its power and form: WordPress as a content-management system. Bucking its blogging roots, WordPress stands as a viable option for library content management needs thanks to new features and excellent usability.

Jones and Farrington introduce readers to the history and progression of WordPress; get you going with the system; help you customize it to your needs; share the best plugins for extending its usability and functionality; and provide a resource list to assist you in your research. Guest pieces from all types of libraries and librarians also grace these pages as exemplary models of and reflections on using WordPress as a content-management system.

I've relied on WordPress for all of my blogging for years and currently use it to create learning communities for my LIS students. Pairing flexibility, stability, and customization with our content, the voices of commenters, and our rich background in organizing knowledge makes WordPress a perfect tool to explore for practically any library's content-management system needs. This report will help guide the way.

Michael Stephens
Assistant Professor, School of Library and
Information Science, San José State University

Preface

Our Goals

As authors of a technical guide we are de facto "tech evangelists." This is an awkward position, for we must constantly fight this interplay in our research, writing, and editing of promoting a tool and, at the same time, acting as its most stout critics. It is one thing to write flippantly and quickly about "the next greatest thing" in library technology; it is quite another to be charged with composing a report that is expected to be read as an unbiased guide.

With this in mind, we have approached this book with a determinedly careful pen, recognizing that our goal within these pages is not to rave about WordPress—you can get plenty of this on WordPress fan sites—but to provide the following for library practitioners:

- A critical overview of WordPress as a web-publishing tool, especially as defined in a content-management system (CMS) context
- An evaluative measure not only of the system's advantageous features but also of any failings that may cause concern or road blocks
- A miscellany of best-of-breed techniques, plugins, and external resources

Content Management Is No Longer Optional

But why even write about another library-related technological tool, especially a CMS? We believe that, now more than ever, content management and strategy as they relate to web publishing have an increased importance in the workflow and identity management of libraries—so much so that they cannot be considered optional. Engaging with library users on the web is no longer restricted to simply putting a static HTML file on a server and calling it a successful website. Yet without technical assistance and forethought, content management can be an actively complex and frustrating process.

Even defining what exactly a CMS is can be daunting. First, how do we define content? Certainly pages and bloglike posts are content, but so are link lists, calendar events, social site updates, image and video galleries, comments, and much more. Each type of content has its own form of authorship and maintenance. And as more content features and types are added into the publishing environment, the CMS becomes even more complex. We define a CMS as follows.

Structurally, a CMS is a type of software application that allows for the online publishing and management of content where content is defined by the author. That content is flexible, extensible, and may exist or be created in a variety of sources but can be somehow interacted with by the CMS.

Organizationally, a CMS promotes content creation by multiple authors via user roles, system permissions, and appropriate and usable publishing interfaces. The opportunity for authors to have varying capabilities as well as work within a usable publishing environment is a sign of a CMS that empowers content creation.

In summary, a CMS is an application that lets you manage your website more efficiently by separating the tasks of designing and managing the website from the job of adding content. Administrative users can configure, customize, and add features to the site; editors/contributors can add, edit, and manage their own contributions without worrying about the more technical aspects of the site.

Library website content must be viewed in much the same way as a physical library's collection:

- Who can access the collection (staff and visitor user roles for the website)?
- What content should be added to the collection (content strategy for publication)?
- Where is the collection accessible (desktop and mobile access to the website)?
- When is the collection accessible (editorial schedule)?
- Why is the collection organized as it is (applying appropriate information architecture and taxonomical systems to content)?
- How is the collection interacted with (social features of the website)?

A library website, to apply S. R. Ranganthan's Fifth Law, is a growing organism and must be treated as such, especially with the complexity of web content. CMSs have been built to handle many, but not all, of the aforementioned needs. Some handle these needs in similar fashions; others take different approaches in technique and complexity.

Creating a Positive (Staff) User Experience

Increasingly, libraries are interested in having multiple authors maintain their website, rather than a single point person. This motivated us to focus our writing and research on how a CMS handles the user experience not only of the website visitor but also, and just as important, of the content creators—that is, the library staff. In her 2010 book *Content Strategy for the Web*, Kristina Halvorson puts it perfectly: "You can buy the Cadillac of all CMSes, with every known feature under the sun, and the implementation can still fail. Why? Because the tool is not the thing. The content and the people who manage it are."

Adding a variety of authors to a library website lends a broader and more human voice to the web presence. Staffers from technical services to administration all experience a unique point of view in the library, not to mention having solidly distinct skill sets. Adding their voices to the collective authorship of the content helps to create a dynamic and engaging website. Doing so, however, increases CMS administration in terms of security practices, user roles, and the online editorial process—all points that must not be overlooked when choosing a CMS.

Once the CMS administration of multiple authors is handled effectively, getting buy-in by staffers to participate in the authoring process is another hurdle to overcome. Although some of this conversation exists in job descriptions and duties outside the scope of this book, the greater point to consider is the content creation experience for the staffers. If it is overly complex or graphically difficult to navigate, staffers will not participate. The importance of massaging the CMS to be friendly to the content creators cannot be overstated.

Starting Your CMS Journey

Choosing a CMS is a process. Extensive testing of CMS candidates is just as vital as vetting them with resources. And do not forget the broad network that is the field of librarianship and the web. Someone, somewhere, either in librarianship or outside of it, has used your particular CMS and most likely has the same questions you have.

No matter which CMS you choose, WordPress should be a strong candidate as you narrow down the field of options. Its extensibility, vibrant community of users, and successful features set it apart from many of its competitors.

Acknowledgments

Kyle M. L. Jones

I'd like to take a few words from this text to thank those who have supported me throughout this writing and who have had an impact on my career in and outside of librarianship:

To my wife, Liz, who now knows more about content types, plugins, and content-management systems than a typical elementary teacher ever should. You were and are an excellent listener even when I talk "geek."

To Michael Stephens, a former teacher of mine, a current friend and colleague, and my advisor emeritus. Your support and advice never go unheard, your friendship is never lost.

To Jacob Hill, the staff, and the rest of the faculty of the A. C. Buehler Library at Elmhurst College, who encouraged me to use their sites as a constant sandbox for exploration with WordPress.

To my coauthor, Polly, my WordPress buddy and fellow technology trainer. Thanks for joining me in this writing quest, for sharing in my frustration and glee, and for bearing with me when my organization and e-mails simply got a little too crazy.

Polly-Alida Farrington

Let me add my words of thanks to the following people:

To my coauthor, Kyle, who generously asked me to join him in this writing project and from whom I have learned an enormous amount about WordPress. It has been a pleasure working with him, and I have appreciated his intelligence, thoughtfulness, patience, and wit throughout this project.

To my good friend and longtime colleague Elaine Baker, who always has the best ideas. In 2006 she hatched a plan to use WordPress to replace the old websites for member libraries in the Southern Adirondack Library System—and then found grant money for us to do it.

And most of all, to my husband, Doug, who listened patiently while I rattled on about WordPress. He is now happily maintaining his own brand-new WordPress site after waiting far too long for me to get around to setting it up for him.

Kyle and Polly

We thank a few groups who have added their knowledge, skill, and support to this project:

Our guest authors, who we knew before we wrote a single word would add a different dynamic to this text than we could offer. We are so thankful that you decided to share your experiences with us and our readers.

We thank the greater WordPress community: from the developers to the theme creators, the community forum participants to the fan sites, your continuous involvement in this CMS is what makes it so great. It's not the tool, it's the people.

And, not forgetting the various cafés and libraries throughout New York, Connecticut, Illinois, and Wisconsin whose caffeine-filled libations and resources—textual, networked, and otherwise—assisted us in the completion of this book.

Part I
Getting Started with WordPress

Multiple Identities
For Blogs, CMSs, and So Much More

WordPress started in 2003 with a single bit of code to enhance the typography of everyday writing and with fewer users than you can count on your fingers and toes. Since then it has grown to be the largest self-hosted blogging tool in the world, used on millions of sites and seen by tens of millions of people every day.

—"About WordPress," WordPress.org

A BRIEF YET INFORMATIVE HISTORY OF WORDPRESS

In 2010, WordPress was powering around 56 percent of all the websites built on CMSs.[1] That's an impressive statistic that speaks not only of WordPress's increasing adoption rate by users but also of its permanence. Millions of individuals across countries and spanning a plethora of disciplines and website purposes have chosen WordPress over such systems as Drupal, Joomla, and ExpressionEngine to house their data, display content, and interact with their site visitors.

But to really grasp how WordPress has risen in the ranks, we need to look a bit into the past to understand where the software has come from and how it might develop in the future. Like most pieces of software, especially those that have gone the open source route, WordPress has a rich history of development.

The Fork, Open Source, Matt, and Automattic

WordPress was not always WordPress. In 2001, b2/cafelog was created by some aspiring individuals who saw a need to develop a web publishing system. Their final project was a piece of blogging software that saw a minimal adoption rate. In 2003, Matt Mullenweg and Mike Little forked the original b2/cafelog code and began what is now known as WordPress. Both b2/cafelog and WordPress were built on the same technical foundations of using open source software tools—MySQL for the database and PHP, a server-side scripting language—to create dynamic pages built on information stored in the database.[2]

For the past nine years of WordPress's existence, and without much of a doubt for its future, it has continued in the open source tradition by unveiling all of the source code it is built on and encouraging community input in its development. From the Codex that holds its technical information to the flurry of activity in the support forums, community involvement is what drives the innovations within WordPress. This would not have been accomplished as successfully without the emphasis on open source.

Who owns WordPress? If a project is truly open source, the community takes responsibility. But a rift of sorts has the community slightly divided. Mullenweg continues as a lead developer of WordPress while maintaining his founder and developer role at Automattic, a venture with over $30 million in funding that runs the highly popular WordPress.com blog host, among other popular applications.[3] The struggle exists in Mullenweg's dual role at WordPress and Automattic, where his influence in the open source organization could be used for his financial gain. Moreover, Automattic employs nine developers (not including Mullenweg) of the WordPress platform, which begs this question: Do they write code that's in the best interest of the community or for Mullenweg's commercial venture Automattic?[4] Though it is easy to raise red flags about this situation, many WordPress supporters believe that Automattic's interest in—if not influence of—WordPress can only add to the stability and improvement of a software package that Automattic relies on for commercial success.

Evolution: Blogs, Specialty Sites, and a Full-Fledged CMS

At the root of WordPress's existence is a firm, consistent focus on the blogging experience. It is the true identity of WordPress and, without hesitation, it must be said that blogging is what WordPress does best before anything else. In fact, WordPress does blogging *so well* that, even when its other features shine and plugins transform it for other purposes, we have heard folks grumble and retort, "It's just a blog." To understand WordPress as a CMS, it is necessary to first identify what makes WordPress such a great blogging system.

Like any good blogging software, WordPress is post-centric, meaning the primary content being published is in post form. Posts are pieces of content—text, media, or a combination of both—that are published in a dynamic manner. They could be written and published for up-to-the minute news, as is the case for Gizmodo's technology liveblog, or in a more traditional daily context, like CNN's Political Ticker. Posts can be scheduled to publish on a certain day and time; they can be set into draft modes for future editing and revision; different draft versions written over time can be compared; and they can be organized in traditional, strictly defined categories or by free-form tagging taxonomy or both. All of this is done in one of the simplest-to-use and most highly regarded user interfaces among competing CMSs.

The team at WordPress wants to make your blogging experience simple and sweet:

> We're never done with simplicity. We want to make WordPress easier to use with every single release. . . . In past releases we've taken major steps to improve ease of use and ultimately make things simpler to understand. . . . We love to challenge ourselves and simplify tasks in ways that are positive for the overall WordPress user experience. Every version of WordPress should be easier and more enjoyable to use than the last.[5]

This dedication to and continual improvement of the user interface and user experience is at the core of why WordPress is one of the most beloved blogging systems—and why it acts as a wonderful framework for unique uses of the software.

What never fails in the WordPress community is someone saying, "I think I can do *x* with WordPress," where *x* is a completely nontraditional approach to what is said to be *just* blogging software. Two excellent examples of such alternative sites just happen to be WordPress community resource sites. One, themefinder (http://themefinder.wpcandy.com), is an aesthetic wonder for visually browsing for WordPress themes by screenshots filtered by color, cost, and layout. In what is still a text-heavy web, themefinder unleashes the potential of creating an entirely visual content experience with faceted searching leading the user to exactly what she wants. In a much different vein, WP Questions (http://wpquestions.com) taps into the WordPress hive mind with a question-and-answer site. The premise: ask a question with a monetary award; pay those who answer your questions most thoroughly and effectively. If more than one individual adds to the overall answer, you can split the reward across responders. All financial transactions are handled quickly and efficiently through PayPal.

It is simple to see that these are dramatically disparate representations of what WordPress can do beyond blogging. They take distinct approaches to defining their content, not to mention to engaging their users in the consumption and creation of the content.

It is ironic when individuals state that WordPress cannot be used as a CMS and then it goes on to win Packt Publishing's 2009 Open Source CMS Award and its 2010 Hall of Fame CMS Award.[6] The "it's just a blog" mentality has permeated most individuals who are on the path to acquiring a new CMS for a project, and the educative process to rectify this idea does take some illustrative effort.

The definition of a CMS, as in our introduction, is truly dependent on the project in which the CMS is used. Generally, though, a site that has some kind of structured content and uses some web-based software to handle that content—as opposed to doing HTML markup by hand—is being powered by a CMS. Two fine academic examples of the use of WordPress as CMS come to mind: those at Bates College (www.bates.edu) and the Tufts Roundtable Commons (www.trcommons.org). Both of these sites have static pages, dynamic blogs, organized media, and a variety of content types to tell stories and provide information about their institutions. Although a cursory glance at the sites doesn't reveal the complexity behind the scenes powered by WordPress, it does suggest that WordPress can and does handle much more than blogs.

Are all of these examples replicable by libraries? Well, that depends. With most visually appealing and pleasing web experiences, a skilled team of developers, information architects, and designers are behind the scenes innovating with the latest programming technologies and implementing industry standards that are proven to create excellent user experiences. It would be foolish to say, "And you can do this, too!" without properly framing such a statement. Some of the aforementioned examples are one-off projects that took great planning and skill to produce and would not be replicable without the same amount of skill by another individual or team. Others, specifically the CMS examples, include elements of content structure and even design which, with effort and time, can be replicated. In fact, the majority of the rest of this book is primarily dedicated to providing the toolbox and resources needed for doing just that.

The Future of WordPress

It is uncertain how WordPress will evolve from here. But if the current trend of innovation in WordPress continues, what we will see could be defined more as a platform for web-based content and user engagement. How does this differ from the current state of WordPress or from CMSs in general? Even with the push for user-generated content, websites—especially library websites—are still very much dependent on their original authors, or owners, for content. As a bona fide platform, WordPress will streamline the process for users as content creators while making the job pleasant.

Beginning with version 1.5, WordPress includes the ability to have any number of users on a site with defined user roles and capabilities.[7] Although this feature has been taken advantage of by select sites, it is still very much a niche case feature. An exceptional example of putting user-created content first and foremost is visible in the P2 Theme (http://p2theme .com). Branded as "Twitter in a box," P2 makes commenting, user status updates, and blogging simple by uncluttering the writing user interface via a front-end editor instead of using an administrative back end. BuddyPress (http://buddypress.org), a comprehensive social networking plugin that adds extensive features to WordPress (see chapter 9), builds on P2 by adding completely customizable user profiles, user groups, forums, and many more social elements. What will be seen in the future of WordPress is a more explicit push—and a streamlined workflow—for user-created content on WordPress sites. And though the current state of WordPress by way of plugins allows for aggregation of content from non-WordPress sites (Twitter, Facebook, et al.) and export of WordPress content such as posts and links, the process can be clunky at times. As more users of WordPress look for flexibility and interoperability of their content from site to site, it can easily be imagined that the contributors to WordPress will hear the call for these features and build them in as native components.

FLAVORS OF WORDPRESS

WordPress.com vs. WordPress.org

When we teach WordPress classes, the most frequently asked question—and a source of great confusion—is about the difference between WordPress.org and WordPress.com.

For many people WordPress.com is their first, and only, experience with WordPress. At WordPress.com you can sign up for a totally free WordPress site. WordPress.com runs the software for you, takes care of upgrades, and maintains the servers. All you have to do is sign up and start adding content. This is one of the services run by Automattic, the company closely allied with the development of WordPress. The free service doesn't allow the complete flexibility had by running the software on your own server, but it's a great place to start experimenting and get a feel for how WordPress works.

The WordPress.org website is home to the WordPress software itself. If you are going to install WordPress on your own web server, download the latest version of WordPress here. WordPress.org is also home to the documentation, WordPress add-ons (themes and plugins), and, most important, the WordPress community, which provides support and a place to share ideas on development of WordPress.

WordPress Single Site vs. WP MultiSite

Prior to the release of WordPress version 3.0 in June 2010, WordPress was available in two "flavors"—single site and multiuser (MU). With the 3.0 release these are now both part of one installation, with the multiuser option now being called MultiSite.

The single-site option is a great choice for running a library or personal website when all the content will be available under a single domain name such as www.mylibrary.org.

The MultiSite option greatly simplifies site administration when a group of separate websites are needed. This is handy for library systems with multiple branches each needing a site with its own subdomain address (e.g., www.eastbranch.mylibrary.org); for special projects that are distinct from the main website (e.g., a special summer reading website or gaming tournament site); or where staff members each want to have their own individual websites.

WE'RE HERE TO HELP: THE COMMUNITY

WordPress comes with a rich community of people and resources you can turn to when you need help. From the forums where beginners ask questions and experts share their advice, to the plugin and theme developers who give of their time and talent and actually listen to the folks who use their tools, to the tutorials, the book authors, the videos, the tweets, the bloggers—there are multitudes of people and resources to help with questions and many opportunities to give back by sharing your expertise.

For a quick jumping-off point, we suggest looking at the Resources section of this publication, which lists a variety of resources including WordPress Codex (the official WordPress documentation site) pages, bloggers, podcasts, and more.

Join the Community

Even if you're just thinking about using WordPress, take the time to join one or more of the support forums, start reading some blogs, or connect with other WordPress users on Twitter, Facebook, and LinkedIn. Lurk for a while and get an idea of how the groups and forums work and which ones you want to be more involved with.

Do Your Homework

No matter how friendly and helpful folks are, no one wants to answer the same question repeatedly. So do your homework before you post a question on a forum or contact a developer:

- Do a web search for the answer to your question. Someone may have already written a blog post about it. If you find an answer, thank them for the help.
- Search the WordPress Codex.
- Search the forums. Again, add a note of thanks if you find the answer.
- If it's a question about a plugin or a theme, check the WordPress.org plugin and theme directories. There are forum pages where plugins and themes are discussed. Also check the developer's website. There may be a forum there as well.
- Read the manuals. The Codex and the variety of WordPress books available are excellent for a range of answers to the questions you may have.

At a Loss?

Post a question on an appropriate forum, but make sure you read the posting rules first; this increases the chances of getting a helpful answer to your question. Explain the problem clearly and thoroughly. Include details such as version numbers, what hosting site you use, and a link back to your site if that will help someone assess the problem. Check back often to see if there are answers, and follow up with any questions asked. If the problem is resolved, post about it so others can learn too. As you gain expertise, watch for opportunities to help someone else.

Fee-Based Support

There are also theme and plugin services that charge for access to their products and support forums. The models vary, some charging a flat fee for a theme or plugin, some charging a monthly fee for support. Paying a little extra to get reliable support when you need it may be a wise investment for many organizations.

A NICE FIT FOR LIBRARIES

Advantages for Libraries and What WordPress Can Do for Them

In our work training library staff to use WordPress websites and in building WordPress websites, we've seen what a perfect fit WordPress is for many types of library and education organizations—large and small. Here are some of the selling points for libraries:

It's free. This certainly is an appealing feature, but it wouldn't be a selling point if WordPress wasn't also such a flexible, full-featured tool for building a dynamic, easy-to-navigate website.

Easy to get started. Once the software is installed on a server, you can build a simple website in just a few hours. The learning curve for WordPress is not daunting.

Web-based administration. Sites can be administered from any computer that has an Internet connection and a browser. You are no longer tied to that one computer that has Dreamweaver (or an outdated version of FrontPage) on it. Now, when a blizzard closes the library, you can log in from home and have up-to-date information on the site.

Share the workload. It is easy to let other people contribute and update content. Set up user accounts for anyone who will be updating the site. There are several different user statuses that help you control who can publish information and who has access to the more powerful administrative features.

Fresh content. Adding a frequently updated news page is simple. News updates (posts) are automatically displayed on either the main page of the site or another page you specify. This keeps your library's online presence fresh and current, with new and interesting content to keep your users coming back for more.

Commenting features. These encourage increased communication with your library's users while providing lots of options for thwarting spam comments.

Flexible and extensible. There are plugins galore that extend the functionality of WordPress. If you find yourself saying, "I wonder if WordPress can do *xyz*," there is likely to be a plugin available that can help. If not, someone with some programming skills can probably create the custom plugin you need.

Remote updating. With apps for various smartphones (Android, iPhone, Blackberry) and devices like the iPad and Android tablets, updating on the go is easy. This is also a great way to stay in touch with any comments being posted on the site and replying quickly.

Some Growing Pains

WordPress continues to grow and improve its strengths while porting in feature requests from the wide community of users. One of the largest and most ambitious of these requests in recent time has been the integration of custom post types (CPTs) in the 3.0 version released in June 2010.[8] Like Drupal's well-developed content construction kit (known widely as CCK), CPTs allow for the creation of content types, like library database and resource lists, through the use of preformatted fields or input areas for content information.

As a new feature, and a feature that will surely grow WordPress's eminence among CMS choices, CPTs are still being fleshed out. CCK's initial release in 2006 most likely went under the same kind of growing pains CPTs are experiencing.[9] Though the ability to create CPTs is built into the underlying code—meaning they are an inherent part of WordPress—they require either a programmer to write PHP to create an actual CPT or a plugin (see chapter 5 for plugin options). Several plugins do exist to do such a job, but the plugin authors are still building in features to fulfill the true potential of CPTs. You can expect CPTs to become a major feature of WordPress in the near future, but understand that their current state is still elementary.

NOTES

1. Matthias Gelbmann, "Highlights of Web Technology Surveys, June 2010: The Amazing Dominance of WordPress as CMS," June 1, 2010, http://w3techs.com/blog/entry/highlights_of_web_technology_surveys_june_2010.

2. Hal Stern, David Damstra, and Brad Williams, *Professional WordPress: Design and Development* (Indianapolis: Wiley, 2010), 2.

3. According to *CrunchBase* (a TechCrunch database), "Automattic," http://www.crunchbase.com/company/automattic, as of 2011.

4. This number was acquired by comparing the developers listed at the WordPress "About" page (http://wordpress.org /about/) and the Automattic "About Us" page (http://automattic.com/about/).

5. "Philosophy," http://wordpress.org/about/philosophy/.

6. "Packt 2009 Open Source Awards," http://www.packtpub.com/open-source-awards-homepage; "2010 Open Source Awards," packtpub.com/open-source-awards-home.

7. "Roles and Capabilities," http://codex.wordpress.org/Roles_and_Capabilities.

8. "Custom Post Types," http://codex.wordpress.org/Custom_Post_Types.

9. "cck 4.7.x-1.x-dev," http://drupal.org/node/96065.

Preparation, Installation, and Initial Settings

LOOK BEFORE YOU LEAP

Before you dive head-on into hosting an installation of WordPress, there a few requirements that you should take note of. None of these are deal breakers—in fact, they are common necessities among most web applications—but you should be sure to ask your web host or system administrator, or, if you are building on your own local computer, check your system settings to see if they are intact and ready for use. We cover two different types of installation environments: a common hosted service by an outside company or department, and a local installation on your own computer.

Technical Requirements

Generally, WordPress requires only two technical elements to be installed: PHP version 5.2.4 or greater, and MySQL version 5.0 or greater.[1] As for servers, WordPress recommends Apache or Nginix, but as long as the server in question can run the previously mentioned versions of PHP and MySQL, the general requirements for installing WordPress are all taken care of.

If the WordPress MultiSite feature is something you know you want to employ straight away or any time in the future, it is absolutely necessary that you consider an additional set of technical requirements. WordPress MultiSite greatly increases the complexity on its server, though not necessarily on site administrators or content creators. The first of these additional requirements is to decide if you want subdirectory sites or subdomain sites. Subdirectories look like extra "folders" on the end of the home site, like so:

http://library.edu/site1

Subdomains seem like pre-sites before a home site, like this:

http://site1.library.edu

Notice the difference of the placement of "site1" either after or before the home site "library.edu"? That placement makes all the difference. If you decide to choose subdirectories for your WordPress MultiSite installation, your server will generally already support this. Simply ask your webhost or system administrator to check and see if the mod_rewrite feature is enabled on your server.

Now, if you prefer that your WordPress MultiSite installation to use the subdomain choice, you need to configure your server to accept wildcards. The WordPress Codex provides a fine example of this two-step process:[2]

- Apache must be configured to accept wildcards.

    a. Open up the httpd.conf file or the include file containing the VHOST entry for your web account.
    b. Add this line:
    ServerAlias *.example.com

- In the DNS records on your server, add a wildcard subdomain that points to the main installation. It should look like:

    A *.example.com

Depending on the server setup at your webhost or institution, using subdomains for your installation of WordPress MultiSite may not be possible. A fine example of this limitation is demonstrated at Dreamhost's user wiki, which requires Dreamhost clients to upgrade to a more costly private server to handle the subdomain technical requirements.[3]

Hosted Services

Free, hosted WordPress services like WordPress.com and EduBlogs.org are a terrific way to get started with WordPress and see how the system works. And it may turn out to be just what you need for your website. Many people run their personal and professional blogs this way.

Free comes at a cost though, in the limitations on what you can do with your site. A major issue for many organizations is not being able to use a professional sounding domain name for their site. For example, all WordPress.com sites have "wordpress.com" as part of their URL (e.g., yourlibrary.wordpress.com).

Most free services display ads on your site as well. They may not be terribly intrusive, but it is still something that is out of your control. Also, though they often provide a wide variety of themes, you are limited to the ones they select. Similarly, you are limited to the add-on features and plugins they support. These are all reasonable restrictions on a free service. But if you plan to create a custom theme and add a lot of plugins, the free services will not meet your needs.

On the plus side, software updates and server maintenance are taken care of for you. This is a huge advantage for many individuals and organizations that want to test the waters and start to see what WordPress can do.

If you like what you see on WordPress.com but really want a custom domain name, take advantage of the premium option to set up a custom domain name for your WordPress.com site.[4] For less than $20 annually, this is a terrific bargain. It gives you a more professional web presence at a rock-bottom price—perfect for cash-strapped libraries that want to create a more engaging, easy-to-update website quickly, easily, and inexpensively. Don't worry, that domain name can be used for a self-hosted WordPress site if you decide to move your site later on. Other premium features offered by WordPress.com include extra storage, ad-free option, and custom CSS. Edublogs.org, which is geared toward the education market, also offers some premium upgrades. These include ad-free sites, easy setup and administration of multiple sites for student use, privacy options, and more.

Pay-for hosting options abound: Dreamhost, Lunar Pages, Rackspace, and similar companies can do the heavy lifting for you with options like one-click installs of WordPress and reliable backups. Of course, their price packages differ, the feature list is never the same, and some may surprise you with hidden limitations (e.g., they support only PHP version 4 or do not allow subdomain installations of WordPress MultiSite). Take your time to examine all the pay-for hosts, just as you would if choosing a free hosted service. Investigate how you might use WordPress for your library and create a technical wishlist; send that wishlist to the support departments of the pay-for host companies. Reputable support services should be happy to talk about your needs, since you are a potential paying customer.

Local Development Environments

Installing WordPress locally—as in on your own desktop computer—to use it as a testing and development environment, is an excellent way to learn the ins and outs of the system without worrying about affecting actual visitors. When you install WordPress in a local development environment, only you can access the site unless you set tweaks to broadcast your site.

Creating a local development environment has valuable benefits:

- You can install any plugin and theme for testing without worrying about its effect on the entire installation. If it breaks something, simply delete it and continue testing.
- You can create any number of users with varying permissions to test authorship and administrative capabilities.
- You can fine-tune the software's settings that will eventually be replicated on your live site.
- Essentially, you can create an entire model of a live site before taking on the stress of maintaining it for access and use by hundreds of thousands of users.

There are combinations of different pieces of software and settings that could be chosen to create a local development environment, but the LAMP, WAMP, and MAMP packages are by far the easiest to set up and the most often recommended. All three packages are considered to be "stacks" of software that use Linux, Windows, or Mac OS X as an operating system, Apache HTTP as the server, MySQL for the database, and PHP for a scripting language (some also include support for Python and Perl). To find out how to get up and running quickly with LAMP, WAMP, or MAMP and WordPress, consult the WordPress Codex "Installing WordPress Locally" section for step-by-step guides.[5]

GET SET, INSTALL!

Part of the beauty of WordPress is how simple it is to get started with the installation process. Honed over many different versions, the WordPress installation process has become so stream-lined that it is known as the "Famous 5-Minute Install."[6] Although this is mostly a branding effort by WordPress to tout its usability, it is fair to say that it is well within the reach of a novice user to install WordPress within five minutes. There are some basic elements of the installation process that need to be completed before the installation. The following steps walk you through the preparation and installation processes with easy-to-follow screenshots.

Preparing Your Database

Whether you are preparing a local installation for testing and development or putting things together for a live site, setting up the database for a WordPress installation is quite simple. For this walk-through we use phpMyAdmin to handle our database creation. Refer to the WordPress Codex site for specific directions for creating a database using popular web hosts' cPanel application.

Creating a database in phpMyAdmin is as simple as choosing a name and clicking Create.

While creating your database be sure to write down the hostname of the database, which may be "localhost" or something like "sql.mysite.com"; the database name that you used in creation of the database; and the user name and password to access the database. You will need all of this information in the near future when you install WordPress.

Downloading WordPress and Moving Your Files

Web hosts like Dreamhost can complete an automated installation of WordPress with a bit of information provided on your part, and although this seems like a time-saving feature, it just pares down a few minutes of work by putting your files in the right place. Since the database is now ready, you can grab the set of WordPress files needed for your installation and move them onto your server via an FTP (file transfer protocol) program or into a local folder if you are building a WordPress site locally.

A note of warning: WordPress.org is the official site for the core set of WordPress files. Never, ever, download this core set of files from anywhere else. They could be altered and could introduce unknown security issues into your server environment or your local computer. You can rest assured knowing that the files provided by WordPress are constantly monitored and updated to address security problems and bugs.

Begin by opening up an Internet browser, pointing it to http://wordpress.org/download, and clicking the "Download WordPress" blue button.

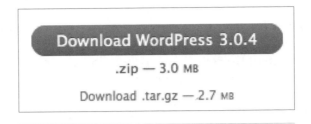

Always download WordPress from the official site.

After the download has completed, open the directory on your server using your FTP application of choice or by opening the local folder for installation if installing locally.
Next, copy the downloaded files into either the server directory or local folder.

Run the Installation

Once all the WordPress files are moved into their proper location, it is all a matter of filling out a simple form that runs the WordPress installation script. With your database information at hand, point your Internet browser to the directory where you copied the WordPress files, fill in the form with the appropriate information, and click Submit.

The simple installation form. Here, a localhost environment is being used and the table prefix has been changed to allow for multiple installations of WordPress in one database.

Final Steps

If WordPress is able to locate the database and install, you are prompted to fill out another simple form to create the first user account, the administrator account. To help further protect your site from potentially hackers, choose a username other than "admin." You can always create more administrative users in the future if need be. If you would like your site to be hidden from search engines like Google and Bing while it is under development, uncheck the privacy option at the bottom of the form. When your site is ready to be released, this setting can be changed from the administrative dashboard.

The final step for installation. Create a username other than "admin" for security and always choose a strong password.

Troubleshooting

Although errors do occur with the installation process, they are typically caused by users filling out the installation form. If you encounter an "error establishing a database connection" message, it usually means one of two things: the information provided to allow WordPress to install necessary information into the database is incorrect, or the server is temporarily inaccessible. Usually rechecking the database credentials and retrying the installation will fix the issues, but you may need to double-check the status of your server with your web host if that is where you are installing WordPress.

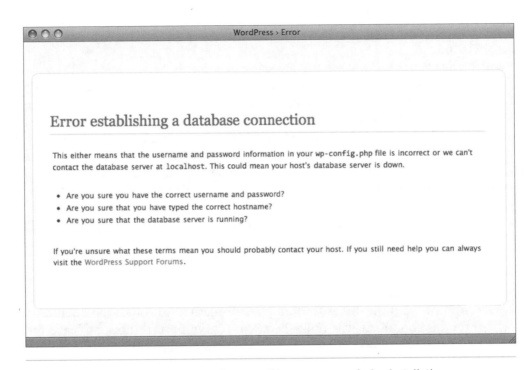

The typical WordPress error message when something goes wrong during installation.

MAKING IT YOURS

Once your server is set up and WordPress is installed, test things by adding a few sample posts and a page or two. And to help you see what your content will look like when it is published, add a test post with all the many HTML elements that will be used on your site. The *Lorelle on WordPress* site has a handy file of HTML that you can copy and paste into a post to show you all the elements.[7]

Next, spend some time reviewing and tweaking the many options in the Settings section of your administrative back end.[8] The sample content you added will help you see what the various options do. These settings control many aspects of how your site works and how users can interact with the content. Settings that are particularly important or might be a bit confusing are explained below.

Note: This section covers only the Settings subpanels that are initially installed with WordPress. Many plugins add their own subpanels to the Settings section, so you may have more subpanels than are covered here.

General Settings

Site title and tagline. The title and tagline you gave the site when you installed WordPress can be edited.

WordPress address and site address. For most installations, these URLs are the same. This option exists for installations where the WordPress files are installed in a subdirectory on the site.

Membership and new user default. If your site has content that will be available only to registered members, use this option to enable the registration features. Note that WordPress does not require people to be members to add comments to a site, so most site owners can ignore this option.

Writing Settings

Size of post box. Default size for the content box on the post and page editing screens. This doesn't limit how much content can be added; it just sets how big the box is. A larger box makes it easier to see what you are editing.

WordPress should correct invalidly nested XHTML automatically. This is intended to help users editing in the HTML code editor by adding opening and closing tags that might have been forgotten. But since it can conflict with some plugins, it is best to leave this unchecked. Ideally, your content contributors will be editing in the WYSIWYG editor and not trying to edit HTML directly.

Press This. Handy tool for including web content in a new post. Drag the Press This link to your browser toolbar, highlight text you want to quote in a post, and click Press This. An editing window appears with the quoted text. Finish editing and publish.

Remote publishing. If you plan to use the WordPress mobile apps or third-party tools such as Scribefire to post to your site, check these boxes.

Update services. In the past, this was an important method to get search engines to notice your new content as soon as it was published. It is less important now, so leave this at the default setting.

Reading Settings

Front Page Displays > Your Latest Posts. By default, WordPress displays news posts on the front page of a site and displays the number of posts you set in Blog Posts Show at Most.

Front Page Displays > A Static Page. Opt for this if you want your main page to contain a welcome page or other static content. But before you change the settings, follow these steps to set up your new home page and news posts page:

Pages > Add New. Create a new page with the content you want on your front page, titling it Home, Welcome, or some other appropriate title.

Pages > Add New. Create another new page without any content and title it News, Updates, or other appropriate title.

Discussion Settings

Default article settings. These settings apply to both posts and pages.

Attempt to notify any blogs linked to from the article. If you refer back to a blog post on another website, WordPress attempts to add a comment on that other post and includes a link back to your post.

Allow link notifications from other blogs. Allows other sites to post a comment on your site when someone references your content.

Allow people to post comments on new articles. Turns commenting on for your site. This can be overridden on individual posts and pages.

Other Comment Settings

Comment author must fill out name and e-mail. This discourages people from posting anonymously and helps prevent some anonymous spam.

Users must be registered and logged in to comment. If your site is a membership-based site, only those who are registered can comment. This is generally not a concern for libraries, though it could be appropriate on educational sites supporting online and classroom learning.

Automatically close comments on articles older than ## days. Spammers often target older posts. This can help cut down on spam.

Enable threaded (nested) comments. Threaded comments can help readers follow replies to comments more easily. Themes differ in their ability to handle comment threading.

Check the navigation bar on your site. Some themes add a default Home link to the top navigation menu, so you may now have two links back to the main page. This can often be fixed by using the Menu feature in the Appearance panel. If your theme does not support the Menu feature, the extra Home link can be deleted by editing the template file that includes the code for the navigation bar. This is often the header.php file, but this can vary from theme to theme. Look for the section that controls the navigation bar. The navigation code is often an *< li >* list and includes the tag wp_list_pages. Often the first *< li >* item in the code is the link to the home page. Take that line of code out and see if it solves the problem. Remember to back up your header.php file in case you need to restore it.

E-mail me whenever. It is best to check both of the settings in this section. This helps you reply to comments in a timely manner without having to spend time visiting your site constantly.

Before a comment appears. These settings often cause confusion. It appears that you can check both boxes, but it is not clear what happens if you do. If you check both boxes, the second option is actually ignored and all comments are held for moderation.

An administrator must always approve the comment. Choose this option if you want to review every message before it appears. But be aware that when comments are not approved quickly your readers may get frustrated and conversations between readers may be stymied. Still, many libraries are concerned about what is said on their sites and feel more comfortable with reviewing all comments before they are published.

Comment author must have a previously approved comment. This is a less restrictive setting. It allows anyone who has already had one approved comment to continue publishing comments without them being held for moderation. One strategy might be to hold all comments for moderation until you get a feel for what types of comments you are receiving and then move to this option.

Comment moderation and comment blacklist. Many spam comments contain long lists of links, so filtering out comments with four or more links can be helpful. The Comment Blacklist lets you block comments based on IP addresses, e-mail addresses, and so forth.

Libraries generally consider carefully how they are going to handle comments and post a simple statement of what is and is not acceptable. Something along the lines of "be courteous and respectful" might be enough. Many libraries that have open comments have found that they do not have problems with inappropriate comments. Remember, we are trying to encourage feedback from our customers and a sharing of ideas. Do what you can to encourage it.

Media Settings

Image sizes. The media settings control default sizes for images inserted into your posts and for media embedded from other sites. When you use the image uploader, WordPress creates three resized images in the sizes specified here: thumbnail, medium, and large. The original image is also retained. If an uploaded image is smaller than the sizes you specify, WordPress does not make a bigger image.

Thumbnail and medium-sized images are displayed on posts and pages and often link users to larger versions of images. So what size to pick? The theme you select influences what sizes to use. Your images should not be so big that they break the layout of your pages. Start testing by uploading and inserting a few images with the default settings and adjust from there. Always check your theme for documentation that specifies what settings to use.

Note: Some themes require square thumbnail images, regardless of the original proportions. If this is the case, check the Crop Thumbnail to Exact Dimensions box to prevent the thumbnail from being distorted to fit into 100 by 100. The medium and large versions will still retain the correct proportions.

Embeds. With WordPress, it is simple to embed videos, photos, polls, and other third-party content in your posts and pages and to specify the maximum size for embedded content. Embedding videos from YouTube, Vimeo, blip.tv, and several other sites is powered by the oEmbed protocol accomplished by simply entering the URL for the video on its own line in a post or page.[9] Example:

```
Check out this great video: http://www.youtube.com/watch?v=-dm_x6EGIHk
```

By default, images are stored in the directory /wp-content/uploads. If needed, you can specify a different directory.

Privacy Settings

When you installed WordPress, you chose whether to make your site public or private. If you change your mind, switch the setting here. If you choose privacy, WordPress adds this code `<meta name='robots' content='noindex,nofollow' />` to the `<head> </head>` section of your content. Visitors can still reach your site via the URL. You may wish to keep your site out of the reach of search engines while you are testing it.

Permalink (URL) Settings

The default URLs for WordPress posts are a bit ugly and not very descriptive. For example, http://yoursite.org/?p = 112 refers to post number 112 and does not tell you anything about when it was published or what it is about. It would be far more useful to have "pretty permalinks" or permanent URLs like these: http://yoursite.org/2011/01/new-hours or http://yoursite.org/news/new-hours. They make more sense to search engines and to human beings.

If your site is running on an Apache web server with mod_rewrite (and most WordPress sites are), you have a file named .htaccess in your root directory. When you reset the Permalink structure, WordPress attempts to write some code to that .htaccess file. If it is successful, you get this confirmation: Permalink Structure Updated. If the .htaccess file is not accessible, the message lists the code you need to add to the .htaccess file by editing the file directly.

Which option to choose? If your site is full of frequent, timely updates, you might want to choose the Month and Name format (/%year%/%monthnum%/%postname%/), which includes the year, month, and post name to help your readers quickly see how current a post is and what it is about (e.g., http://yoursite.org/2011/01/new-hours).

If your updates will be less frequent and not as tied to particular dates, a custom structure with a fixed label to be used for all news posts followed by the post name (/news/%postname%/) may be useful (e.g., http://yoursite.org/news/research-tips).

The content in %postname% is created from the title you give each post. As you type a post, the title is used to create the permalink. This can be edited from the permalink line that appears right under the title when you are editing a post.

All of the possible permalink structure tags can be found in the WordPress Codex.[10]

Though you can change your permalink structure after your site has been running for a while, it can be confusing to users (and search engines) who have links to the old URLs. That said, WordPress can redirect users to the new pages, but apparently it can remember only back to the last change, so changing your link structure multiple times results in broken links. It is best to avoid changing at all, by experimenting with the settings before your site goes live.

GET YOUR CAPE AND FANCY SPANDEX, YOU'RE NOW A SUPER ADMIN

One of the most anticipated features for WordPress version 3.0 was the merging of two different WordPress platforms: regular WordPress and WordPress MU. Whereas WordPress handles only one site, WordPress MU was able to use a single installation of WordPress but create a nearly infinite number of subsites. In fact, the MU version was so successful at scaling that it could support the millions of blogs and hundreds of thousands of active users at the site. Now, it is doubtful that libraries will create a publishing environment of that magnitude, but it is entirely possible that they would like to have multiple sites with one easy-to-use installation.

Background on MultiSite

WordPress MU is no longer, but its legacy lives on in WordPress 3.0 and newer versions in a feature called MultiSite. When enabled, MultiSite turns on the following capabilities:

- New administrative user role called Super Admin
- Ability to create new sites and users for those sites in a few keystrokes
- Control over what themes are visible throughout the network of sites
- Specific MultiSite options regarding user registration, new site settings, upload capabilities, and more
- Ability to upload the entire MultiSite network with a click of a button

Some of the beauty involved with MultiSite is that an administrator with no previous Multi-Site experience can pick up the new features and responsibilities quickly because of the intuitive options and interface.

Enabling MultiSite on your WordPress installation requires a certain finesse. In the early stages of WordPress 3.0 development, a turnkey feature was built in to enable MultiSite with a click of a button, in typical WordPress style. Unfortunately, concerns arose regarding unaware WordPress users and the responsibilities they would be undertaking if they accidentally turned on MultiSite and the feature was removed. Because of this possibility, MultiSite takes a little technical tweaking to get it working. We cover the details of this later on in this section, but there is an easy way to get MultiSite up and running: with a plugin, of course.

The Easy Way

Enable MultiSite is a simple-to-use plugin that takes some of the stress and struggle away from having to actually enable MultiSite the way WordPress prefers: by editing your configuration file. To download Enable MultiSite, use the built-in plugin installer within your site or download the plugin from the WordPress plugin repository.[11] Be sure to enable the plugin after download.

Go to the settings options and choose the new Enable MultiSite option. Before continuing, back up your database and all of the files for your WordPress-enabled website. Enabling MultiSite via the plugin or by hand as instructed here alters configuration files and makes necessary adjustments to your database. As a precaution, you should back up these items in case something were to go wrong—although in our experience of setting up many a MultiSite installation, rarely anything does.

Now you are presented with a form to fill out and an option regarding subdomain or subdirectory installs. If you are a little fuzzy on the difference between subdomain and subdirectory installs, refer back to the "Look Before You Leap" section that opens this chapter. Making the right choice is pivotal. After you submit the form, your installation is complete. Simply log in again, and you are able to access the MultiSite features by clicking on "My Sites" at the top of the dashboard screen.

Welcome to the Network installation process!

Fill in the information below and you'll be on your way to creating a network of WordPress sites. We will create configuration files for you.

Addresses of Sites in your Network

Please choose whether you would like sites in your WordPress network to use sub-domains or sub-directories. **You cannot change this later.**

You will need a wildcard DNS record if you are going to use the virtual host (sub-domain) functionality.

- ◉ Sub-domains   like site1.mylibrary.dev and site2.mylibrary.dev

- ○ Sub-directories   like mylibrary.dev/site1 and mylibrary.dev/site2

Network Details

Server Address   The internet address of your network will be mylibrary.dev .

Network Title   My Library Sites
               What would you like to call your network?

Admin E-mail Address   library_admin@mylibrary.org
               Your email address.

Install

The form for finalizing your MultiSite configuration.

The Hard Way

Using the Enable MultiSite plugin does all the heavy lifting for you, but on the off chance that the plugin is not up to speed with the latest version of WordPress (or you simply like to do things by hand), knowing how to do the technical walk-through could come in handy. As with the plugin, make sure your database and site files are backed up. Open the wp-config .php file in your website's home directory and type the following line:

```
define('WP_ALLOW_MULTISITE', true);
```

Be sure to put that right above this line near the bottom of the file:

```
/* That's all, stop editing! Happy blogging. */
```

Now, if you have not logged in to your website, do so and head to the Tools menu to see a new option titled Network. As with the plugin, simply fill out the form and click install. Next you find a rather forbidding screen of code. Don't fret. Follow the simple directions to create the blogs.dir folder in wp-content and add the appropriate lines to the wp-config.php file you already have edited.

That final box is the tricky one. Files that begin with a period, like .htaccess, are invisible on most operating systems and FTP applications. Open your favorite text editor, paste in the text for the .htaccess file it would like you to create, and—this is important—save that file as "htaccess.txt." Once you place that file in the home directory of all your WordPress files for your site, simply rename it ".htaccess." It most likely will "disappear"—and that's okay. The operating system or FTP application is doing what it does—hides files with periods at the beginning of file names. Once this is done, log in again to your site and you are granted Super Admin privileges with your MultiSite network enabled.

NOTES

1. "Requirements," http://wordpress.org/about/requirements/.
2. "Setting Wildcard Subdomains," http://codex.wordpress.org/Create_A_Network#Step_2_Setting_Wildcard _Subdomains.
3. "WordPress MU," http://wiki.dreamhost.com/WordPress_MU.
4. "Domain Mapping," http://en.support.wordpress.com/domain-mapping/.
5. "Installing WordPress Locally," http://codex.wordpress.org/WordPress_Installation_Techniques#Installing_Word Press_Locally.
6. "Famous 5-Minute Install," http://codex.wordpress.org/Installing_WordPress#Famous_5-Minute_Install.
7. "WordPress Post Content Sandbox Content Updated," http://lorelle.wordpress.com/2009/01/17/wordpress-post -content-sandbox-content-updated/.
8. "WordPress Codex: Administration Panels" http://codex.wordpress.org/Administration_Panels#Settings.
9. For a full list of services that can be embedded with this method, see "WordPress Codex: Embeds," http://codex .wordpress.org/Embeds.
10. "WordPress Codex: Using Permalinks," http://codex.wordpress.org/Using_Permalinks#Structure_Tags.
11. "Enable MultiSite," http://wordpress.org/extend/plugins/wordpress-multi-site-enabler-plugin-v10/.

Part II
Full-On Customization with Themes and Plugins

Extensibility via Plugins

NEEDS AND WANTS

Plugins extend what WordPress can do, and they can be created by anyone with some coding skills. With over 12,000 plugins in the official WordPress.org plugin directory (http://wordpress.org/extend/plugins/), there are a lot of additional features you can add to your site. Need a contact form? A way to back up your data? An event calendar? A spam catcher? Yep, there are plugins for all those and more.

Although plugins are wonderfully handy, the more you install, the more likely you are to run into a conflict that could cause problems. Consider carefully whether you really *need* a particular plugin or you just *want* it. Plugins sometimes just make simple changes that you could also accomplish by editing your functions.php, CSS, or theme files—but only if you are comfortable working with code.

So how, exactly, do you begin? Take your first step by *not* searching for any plugins— just yet. You save yourself time and headaches by creating a plugin wishlist that takes these questions into consideration before choosing a plugin:

- What should the plugin's purpose be?

    Does it create content?
    Does it improve site administration?
    Does it help the user experience?

- What is the end goal of the plugin?

    Is it to improve the commenting features?
    Is it to allow e-mails to be sent to the site administrator?

Is it to improve the site's connectivity with social media the library uses?
Is it to make administration of the site easier?

- What are you willing to dedicate to the plugin in terms of time?

  If the plugin requires someone to work with it constantly, are the resources available?
  If the plugin is new, are you willing to update it more than others as bugs arise and new features are rolled out?
  Though it is safe to say that many of the plugins available are "plug-and-play," are you prepared to do a moderate amount of testing and tweaking to meet your goals?

FINDING THE RIGHT PLUGIN

Part of the beauty of extending WordPress as a CMS is choosing the absolute best-fit combination of plugins that accomplish your content goals and administrative needs. The process is exciting—and mostly enjoyable as you fine-tune your setup—but your beginning steps are fraught with the daunting challenge of choosing from more than 12,000 different plugins. And that's just at the WordPress plugin repository. Premium plugins are sold by developers on their own, adding to the WordPress repository of freely available plugins.

Now that your wishlist is set, put your masterful search skills to use by digging through the WordPress plugin repository. Don't get overwhelmed by the quantity of plugins available. Know that you need to dedicate some search time to finding a set of plugins that may work for your specific need.

There are five different filters for searching for plugins: by relevance, by newest added to the repository, by recently updated, by most popular, and by highest rated. Each filter has its advantages, but we suggest using the default relevance feature, which provides the best fit for your search term. Although the popularity and ranking filters sound similar, they are not: popularity is based on amount of downloads, and ranking is selected by users. You can safely bet that the popularity filter is a greater indicator of the plugin's success over the user ranking—which is highly subjective and spotty at best. We have used many plugins that work wonderfully but have no or low rankings. Do your part for the WordPress community: rank those plugins you use and test so as to enhance the quality of these ratings.

Once you have selected a potential plugin for use in your site, be sure to be thorough in checking out its description:

- Check that it will work with your version of WordPress.
- Read the documentation: Are there any special requirements the plugin needs?
- Check the version history and how recently the plugin has been updated—both are good indicators of how active the plugin developer is.

Making these simple checks helps cut down on testing and debugging as you build your plugin framework on which to extend WordPress as a CMS.

It cannot be said enough that testing a plugin is essential. In the best-case scenario you use a testing environment—an installation of WordPress other than your live site—that you can run plugins on without affecting visitors and staff who are working on the site. The worst-case scenario is that a plugin causes a critical issue with your site, providing you with what is commonly called in the WordPress community "the white screen of death." This is quite a misnomer, for nothing has "died." Simply delete the plugin from the wp-content directory wherever your site is installed and refresh your browser. Clearly, in this case the plugin had some technical issues or conflicted with another plugin. In a still-not-so-wonderful scenario, a plugin could work but you just need some customizing of either your theme or the plugin's settings to get the optimum result. See why a testing environment might be a good thing to use?

If the WordPress plugin repository fails to provide you with the optimum plugin solution, look to premium plugin developers. For a great starting point for finding these sellers of plugins, look at the resource section at the end of this publication. Prices for premium plugins vary but usually include additional documentation and support for purchasing the plugin along with their exceptional features.

There is a sentiment among some users and administrators of open source CMSs that purchasing additional elements—like plugins and themes—is somehow antithetical to using open source software. The opinion is understandable, but don't let it deny you the opportunity to enhance your overall WordPress setup. Sometimes a premium plugin is just better designed and has more features than its free counterpart—and at prices like $25 and $40, they are relatively cheap.

While on the topic of cost, think, if you will, of the amount of time, effort, and skill that goes into creating some of the amazing plugins available for free. If your budget allows, consider donating any sum of money to the developer. Without a doubt, they will greatly appreciate it.

To donate to the developer, look for the "Donate to this plugin" link in the FYI box within each plugin's page.

Look and Feel with Themes

SEPARATING CONTENT FROM DESIGN

When you create content for your site, whether a news update, a page of library information, or a list of links to great research resources, the content is stored in a database without any information about how and where to display it.

Content stored in your database can then be used in a variety of ways. For example, a page listing the most recent news posts can take the latest ten post titles and the first sentence from the post to create a teaser page. And each post can also have its own individual page that has the title, full contents, and other data related to the single post. Similarly, a list of the latest headlines might appear on the sidebar of your pages to give people easy access to the latest news. All of that information is stored in the database just once but is being used over and over in different places.

It is a site's theme that controls which information appears where and what it looks like. Themes make your content look good. Without theme files, WordPress just wouldn't know how to display your content on the screen.

What Is a Theme?

A theme is a collection of files that creates the structure and design of your site. A theme consists of template files (index.php, header.php, etc.) that control the structure and layout of your pages and cascading style sheet (CSS) files (style.css) that define the colors, fonts, and styles and generally make everything look great.

By separating content (stored in the database) from the structure and design (controlled by themes), WordPress and other systems provide a flexible framework for website development. If you want to tweak the look of your site, just make changes to the theme files. Want to redesign the site completely? Choose a new theme or create your own theme. All your content remains the same; it is just displayed differently. When we started writing HTML we couldn't even dream of such a flexible way to create a website. We wonder what another twenty years will bring?

How Do Themes Work?

At a minimum, a theme must include these two files:

index.php. The default template file that specifies what information to include on the page and where to display it. Most themes include additional template files for pages that need a different layout.

style.css. The CSS code that makes your content look good. This includes information about colors, fonts, sizes, margins, background colors, and so forth.

Some other common files are header.php, sidebar.php, footer.php, comments.php, and search .php. Each of these files contains code to display a particular piece of a WordPress page. They all work together to create the pages you see on your site. For example, if you take a look at the code in a theme's index.php file, you likely see a line of PHP code that looks like something like this:

```
<?php get_header(); ?>
```

That pulls in the code from the header.php file to create the header on the page. So if you want to edit something in the header area of your site, you need to edit the header.php file. Look through the file and you see similar code that displays the sidebar and footer. Don't be put off by the PHP code in the files. You don't need to be a PHP pro to use WordPress, though it can't hurt to learn a bit about it.

Appearance Panel

The Appearance administration panel is where you select a theme for your site, search for and install new themes, customize the sidebar content with widgets, build navigation menus, and edit theme files.

Selecting a Theme

In the Appearance > Themes subpanel you find previews of the themes that are currently installed on your server. Themes are stored in the wp-content/themes/ subdirectory on your server, each theme in its own subdirectory (e.g., wp-content/themes/twentyten).

To preview a theme, click on the theme image or the Preview link. The preview gives you a good idea of what your content will look like if you activate the theme. To give the theme a thorough test, use the Activate link to apply the theme to your whole site. When you are just getting your site set up, you spend a lot of time preview and testing themes.

Adding New Themes

At the top of the Appearances > Themes subpanel, select the Install Themes tab. From this panel you can search for themes in the WordPress.org Free Themes Directory (http://word press.org/extend/themes/) by keyword, colors, layout style, and a variety of other features.

You can also browse for featured, newest, and recently updated themes. To install a theme, click on the Install link, then the Install Now button in the preview window.

Use the Upload option to install themes that have been downloaded from sources other than the WordPress.org directory. Though themes are usually distributed as .zip files, you don't need to unzip the file before using the upload option. However, if you're using FTP to move the files directly to your server, you do need to unzip them first.

Editing Theme Files

The Appearance > Editor subpanel gives you access to all of the files contained in each theme. The files for the active theme are displayed by default. Select a file from the list on the right, and the code appears in the big text box where it can be edited.

The .php files contain a combination of PHP code and HTML. PHP interacts with your database content and calls up various WordPress functions, and the HTML defines the structure of the page. Though you don't need to know everything about PHP and HTML, you do need to recognize which is which when you edit files. If you make a mistake editing the PHP code, you are like to get a scary "fatal error" message when you look at your site. Always make backup copies of the files.

Blocks of PHP code begin with `<?php` and end with `?>` (e.g., `<?php get_search_ form(); ?>`). HTML is composed of paired tags and text like `<h1>This is a heading </h1>`.

If the idea of editing one of these .php files seems a bit daunting, try your hand at editing the 404.php file. This file creates the "404 file not found" page. If you are working on a test site that is not yet public, go ahead and try out the file editor found in the Appearance options panel. And whether it is a test site or a live site, make sure you make a backup of your theme files before you edit. That way you can always restore the original file if you need to.

Look for the message somewhere in the middle of the code that looks something like this:

```
<div class="entry-content">
  <p>
    <?php _e( 'Sorry, page not found. ',
  'themename' ); ?>
  </p>
</div>
```

Change the message and save the file. Then test it out by trying to visit a nonexistent page in your site.

If your 404 page does not have a search box on it, you can add one by adding this code under the message you just edited:

```
<div class="entry-content">
  <p>
    <?php _e( 'Sorry, page not found. ',
  'themename' ); ?>
  </p>
  <?php get_search_form(); ?>
</div>
```

Theme-Specific Settings

Though you can customize themes by editing the CSS and PHP layout files, many theme designers include options for customizing the look and feel of a theme through easy-to-use administration panels. Generally you find theme-specific options somewhere in the

Appearances administration panel, but they may be in other sections of the dashboard. The options available vary widely from theme to theme.

Other than making it easy to customize, this approach can also save all of your custom settings in a file that is not overwritten when the theme is upgraded. This way the theme author can tweak, update, and add new features to the theme without losing all your customizations. Not all themes actually work this way, so do read the theme's documentation.

"Sidebars Are for 'Stuff'": Widgets

"Sidebars are for 'stuff.' . . . We don't want this stuff in the footer because that's way down there all lonely at the bottom of the page. So we put it on the side instead. Stuff = alternative navigation, ancillary content, small forms, descriptive text, advertising, blogrolls, pictures of cats . . . stuff."[1] And widgets are how we get that stuff onto the sidebars. Widgets are little boxes that can be placed in various sidebars on your sites. Most themes have at least one sidebar, usually a narrow column on the left or right side of the page, and sometimes on both sides of the page. It's a bit more accurate to call these areas "widget areas," since theme designers have been building themes with customizable widget areas in the header and footer areas as well.

Widgets provide lots of ways to customize a site. They can contain all sorts of content. Widgets with a list of recent news posts, recent comments on the site, and links to various pages on the site can help your readers find their way to other content. Widgets can also display content from other websites, an RSS feed of news from your local newspaper, a stream of photos from your library's Flickr account, your library's Twitter updates, listings of new material from your library catalog, and so on.

> By default, the basic sidebar in a new WordPress installation has three widgets on the sidebar: Search, Archives, and Meta. As soon as you add more widgets to the sidebar, those three disappear from the sidebar. If you do want them to reappear, just drag them back onto the sidebar.

Widgets are preconfigured to handle particular types of content and usually have some configuration options. For example, the Recent Posts widget creates a list of the most recent news posts from your site. You decide how many posts and what that box of content is to be called.

Open the Appearance > Widgets subpanel and explore the list of widgets available to you. Some widgets are there by default in all WordPress installations, and others have been added by the various plugins your site is using.

The sidebars available in your theme are shown on the right. Drag a widget to one of the sidebars and expand it to see the customization options. You can use a widget as many times as needed. For example the RSS widget could be placed on the sidebar multiple times, each instance pulling in content from a different RSS feed.

There are two types of widgets here:

Available Widgets. These are widgets that haven't been configured yet.

Inactive Widgets. These are widgets that you have removed from a sidebar and want to reuse later. The settings you configured are retained.

Some popular widgets:

Text. An incredibly useful blank box. You can put any sort of text and HTML code in this widget. List your library hours, address, and phone number—an easy way to display contact info on every page. Highlight an upcoming event. Add a graphic and link to one of your databases or e-book services.

Search. Adds a search box to search the site.

Links. Lists of links that you have added in the Links content panel.

RSS. Anything that has an RSS feed can be pulled into your site with this widget: latest headlines from a news source, Twitter feed, headlines from a popular blog, book reviews, list of new materials in the catalog.

Custom Menu. Places custom navigation menus on the sidebar.

Archives. Menu to help readers find news posts from a particular month.

Categories. List of all the topics you have assigned to your news posts. Helps readers find content on the topics they are interested in.

The default widgets provide many ways to add content to your sidebar, and as you add new features to your site through the use of plugins, you'll see even more widgets appearing in this panel.

Menus

Many themes have a default navigation bar/menu somewhere across the top of the pages. In the past, these navigation bars usually just contained links to the main pages in your site. And though it was possible to customize the navigation, it was not a straightforward process.

With the new Menus feature in WordPress 3.0, it is now easy to build custom navigation menus with links to any combination of pages, topic categories, specific posts, external links, and more. Although some themes don't yet support this feature, the number of themes that do is growing. Even if a theme doesn't fully support the new feature, you can still build custom menus and use the Custom Menu Widget to place them on the sidebars of your site.

Open the Appearance > Menus panel to find out if your theme supports Menus and to see what options you have.

Building a Custom Menu

On the left side of the Menus subpanel, there are lists of the pages and categories used in the site. There is also a box for creating Custom Links, which are handy for linking to your library's catalog and other external resources. If you created any Custom Post Types or Custom Taxonomies, these are also displayed.

- Name your menu and click on Create Menu.
- Select the various items you want in your menu and Add to Menu.
- Add any Custom Links.
- Items can be rearranged by dragging the boxes around in the Menu panel.
- To create submenus, just drag one item onto another.
- In the Theme Locations box, select your new menu to assign it to the navigation for the site.

Custom Menus and the Custom Menus Widget

If your theme does not fully support the Custom Menus feature, you can still build menus to appear on the sidebars:

- Build your menus as detailed above.
- In the Appearance > Widgets panel, drag the Custom Menu widget to the sidebar.
- Expand the widget, add a name, and select the Custom Menu you want on the sidebar.

Taking Themes Further: Child Themes

It is not unusual when looking for a theme to find one that is *almost* perfect, a theme that with just a little tweaking would be just what you need. With WordPress, you can make changes to the template files and CSS code and make a theme your own.

But what happens when the original theme gets updated with some really great features that you want to take advantage of, but you still want to retain all the changes you have made? If you upgrade the theme, it will overwrite your customized versions of the files, and there go your changes.

Creating a child theme solves this problem. Using this strategy, you create a new theme that contains all of the changes you need. That theme includes code that connects the child theme back to the parent theme. Basically, the child theme says to use the templates and CSS from the parent theme unless there is something in the child theme that overrides the parent theme.

An example: Let's say you love the default WordPress theme called TwentyTen, but you want to change the text color for the site description at the top of all the pages.

- Create a new theme folder on your server, and name it twentytenchild.
- Create a text file called style.css.
- Include the following text at the start of the style.css file:

```
/*
   Theme Name: twentytenchild
   Description: A Child Theme of TwentyTen
   Author: your name here
   Template: twentyten
*/
```

The Theme Name is the name you give to your child theme (required). The Description is an optional description of your theme. Also optionally, you can add your name as Author. The Template is the directory that holds the parent theme—case sensitive (required).

Unless you are creating a completely new set of styles for your site, refer back to the styles in the parent theme. To load those styles, add this line of code:

```
@import url("../twentyten/style.css");
```

Then start adding your own styles; in this example, the text for the site description is designed to be red (#f00) and bold.

```
#site-description {
   color: f00;
   font-weight: bold;
}
```

That complete style.css file now looks like this:

```
/*
Theme Name: twentytenchild
Description: A Child Theme of TwentyTen
```

```
Author: your name here
Template: twentyten
*/
@import url("../twentyten/style.css");
#site-description {
  color: f00;
  font-weight: bold;
}
```

Put the style.css file in your new twentytenchild directory, return to the Themes panel, and activate your new theme.

When working with themes and CSS files, it helps enormously to install tools to help you identify which pieces of CSS code are used to format the different sections of your site: Two popular toolbars are Webdeveloper for Firefox and Chrome (http://chrispederick.com/work /web-developer/) and FireBug (http://getfirebug.com).

FINDING THE RIGHT THEME

The appearance of your sites means a lot to you, or if it doesn't, it should. The design of your site represents your library, your staff, your collection, and you. Simply put, it is like your logo—except much more complex. It is part art and part function: the colors, lines, fonts, graphics, and gradients have to complement the content that needs to get to the site visitor. So in choosing a theme you are met with some formidable choices.

Sometimes web design and information architecture are pushed to the wayside for the "I want/need a new/better website" mentality. Yet this rush for a website ignores the fact that usability testing and artistic skills dictate what a website should look like and how it should be structured cosmetically. We urge you—no matter your CMS—to consider this before putting the "clothes," so to speak, on your website. By doing so you are able to consider the following when choosing a theme:

- Structural elements: one column, two columns, three columns, header and footer spaces
- Graphical choices: gradients, repeating images, contrasting or complementary colors
- Typography: serif, sans serif, browser-supported fonts, preloaded fonts, Google-hosted fonts

Luckily for those who choose WordPress for their website needs, its free theme choices are far superior in quantity than some comparable open source CMSs. More than 1,300 themes are available at the WordPress theme repository.[2] And, like plugins, this isn't even mentioning the premium themes available at extraordinarily low costs and high quality.

In a much improved fashion over the WordPress plugin repository, the theme repository has an excellent tag-and-filter faceted search process to find the theme that meets your needs.[3] There are five ways to filter your results with accompanying options: by color (five options), by column (six options), by width (two options), by features (thirteen options), and by subject (three options).

As when you test plugins, you should test your theme choices in an environment other than your live site. Whereas plugins bring the possibility of severe conflicts that could temporarily bring down your site and disrupt your visitors, switching themes on them mid-visit will simply confound them. Use your test environment to see how theme choices affect the display of your content. You can run the theme through its paces by completing these steps:

1. Add several pages of test content (if need be, use the "lorem ipsum" text generator to create some fake text for the pages: http://www.lipsum.com).

2. Add several test posts.

3. Assign categories to your test posts. And tags, if you plan to use them.

4. Add comments to some of those posts.

5. If the theme has special page templates, give all of them a test with some "lorem ipsum" as well.

6. Work through the theme's specially created settings.

You will probably end up switching back and forth between themes several times as you compare.

If you have questions about how a theme works, consult any documentation that might be available from the theme developer and check the wordpress.org forums for any discussion of the theme. Don't worry about the things you can change, like colors and font styles. These can be changed by editing the themes styles.css file. Pay more attention to page layouts and options, aspects that aren't as easy to change.

If the WordPress theme repository has nothing to your liking, you are left with two options: purchase a premium theme, or create your own. The former is by far the simplest option. Premium theme creators are abundant and priced well below what they should be, considering their quality. These themes come packed with options for customization and unique ways to present content. A fine selection of premium theme creators is available in the resource section of this book.

With knowledge of PHP, HTML, CSS, and some research on WordPress's own template tags, creating a custom theme is not out of reach.[4] Understand, though, that this is quite an undertaking and can become quite an intense project for someone not as well versed in PHP as in HTML and CSS. An additional option is to purchase a premium theme framework, which, as the name suggests, creates a framework or blank canvas full of WordPress-specific and general theme options but without the colors, images, and overall branding involved in web design. The resource section also lists some popular frameworks available for purchase.

NOTES

1. Coyier and Starr, *Digging into WordPress* (2011), 74.

2. "Free WordPress Themes," http://wordpress.org/extend/themes/.

3. "Tag Filter," http://wordpress.org/extend/themes/tag-filter/.

4. "Template Tags," http://codex.wordpress.org/Template_Tags.

Part III
WordPress Cookbooks:
Tips, Tricks, and Plugins

A Better Workflow

FOR ADMINISTRATORS

Administrating a site of any size and complexity is a tough project, but as the level of content increases, varieties of user roles are created, and as plugins are included to increase functionality, the responsibility of the site administrator increases exponentially. To handle that extensive duty successfully and as stress free as possible, multiple plugins could be employed to ease the pain of site administration.

The following plugins increase administrative functionality in a variety of ways: WP Maintenance Mode pulls a site down temporarily while updates are being made; the Theme and Plugin Visibility Manager plugins allow site administrators to limit who has access to what theme and plugin; Role Scoper and User Role Editor allow the administrator to create, edit, and limit user roles; Admin Menu Editor helps to reorganize the administrative panels and limit (or enable) access to certain settings pages based on user roles; and Adminimize lets the administrator target specific elements, all the way down to targeted CSS IDs and classes of all settings screens, and hide them based on particular roles. Some of the plugins may repeat certain types of tasks, but it is important to note how they approach different settings and additions to the overall functionality of the system. Always test plugins and combinations of plugins to figure out which one or ones work best for your particular setup.

WP Maintenance Mode

http://wordpress.org/extend/plugins/wp-maintenance-mode/
There are times when your site needs to go down for scheduled periods for maintenance. Instead of having visitors see a blank white screen, using a plugin like WP Maintenance Mode makes that experience informational. WP Maintenance Mode allows you to create a styled theme for your splash page, including a countdown until the site goes back live.

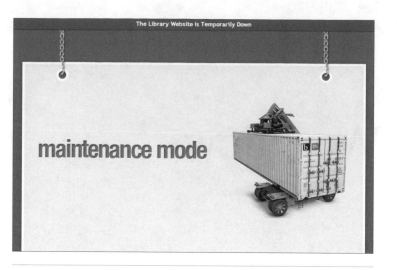

An example splash page enabled by the WP Maintenance Mode plugin.

Theme Visibility Manager

http://wordpress.org/extend/plugins/theme-visibility-manager/
If you are managing a WordPress MultiSite installation, you may find yourself with multiple themes installed, especially if you are allowing any user to create a blog, as might be the case for a community site. On the same installation you might be hosting the central library website. In a situation like this you don't want a community site to have access to your library's theme. Theme Visibility Manager limits which themes are and are not accessible by default.

Global theme visibility management						
Themes must be enabled for your network before they will be available to individual sites, whether "shown" through this plugin or not. Go here to network-enable themes.						
☐ Theme	Version	Description		Network-enabled?	Show	Hide
☐ Twenty Ten	1.1	The 2010 theme for WordPress is stylish, customizable, simple, and readable — make it yours with a custom menu, header image, and background. Twenty Ten supports six widgetized areas (two in the sidebar, four in the footer) and featured images (thumbnails for gallery posts and custom header images for posts and pages). It includes stylesheets for print and the admin Visual Editor, special styles for posts in the "Asides" and "Gallery" categories, and has an optional one-column page template that removes the sidebar.		Yes	Globally Show	Globally Hide
☐ Theme	Version	Description		Network-enabled?	Show	Hide

The settings page for the Theme Visibility Manager plugin.

Plugin Visibility Manager

http://wordpress.org/extend/plugins/plugin-visibility-manager/
Much like Theme Visibility Manager, Plugin Visibility Manager limits who has access to what plugins. Site administrators need to pay special attention to the kind of access nonsystem administrators have to plugins, since some have amazing settings that transform WordPress installations. Unwanted access and accidental setting changes could drastically affect how a site works.

Global plugin visibility management

This page can globally, i.e. for every blog on the site, make visible or hide plugins. Simply click on the links below and to the right to enforce site-wide plugin visibility policies. The changes go into effect immediately.

	Plugin	Version	Description	Visible	Hidden
☐	Add Logo to Admin	1.3.3	Adds a custom logo to your site's Admin header and your login page.	Globally Show	Globally Hide
☐	Adminimize	1.7.12	Visually compresses the administrative meta-boxes so that more admin page content can be initially seen. The plugin that lets you hide 'unnecessary' items from the WordPress administration menu, for alle roles of your install. You can also hide post meta controls on the edit-area to simplify the interface. It is possible to simplify the admin in different for all roles.	Globally Show	Globally Hide
☐	Admin Menu Editor	1.0.1	Lets you directly edit the WordPress admin menu. You can re-order, hide or rename existing menus, add custom menus and more.	Globally Show	Globally Hide
☐	After The Deadline	0.49007	Adds a contextual spell, style, and grammar checker to WordPress. Write better and spend less time editing. Visit your profile to configure. See the Proofreading Support page for help.	Globally Show	Globally Hide
☐	Akismet	2.4.0	Akismet checks your comments against the Akismet web service to see if they look like spam or not. You need an API key to use it. You can review the spam it catches under "Comments." To show off your Akismet stats just put `<?php akismet_counter(); ?>` in your template. See also: WP Stats plugin.	Globally Show	Globally Hide
☐	All in One SEO Pack	1.6.13	Out-of-the-box SEO for your Wordpress blog. Options configuration panel | Upgrade to Pro Version | Donate | Support | Amazon Wishlist	Globally Show	Globally Hide

The settings page for the Theme Visibility Manager plugin.

Role Scoper

http://wordpress.org/extend/plugins/role-scoper/
A highly popular program among WordPress administrators, Role Scoper enhances access to the inherent roles and capabilities built into the software by allowing administrators to change permissions on granular levels. Role Scoper also supports custom post types and taxonomies.

Role Scoper settings for restricting access to posts based on specific roles.

User Role Editor

http://wordpress.org/extend/plugins/user-role-editor/
Like a pared-down Role Scoper, User Role Editor provides a quick and simple interface for adding roles and editing built-in roles.

User Role Editor uses a simple checkbox system to add or take away capabilities from roles.

Admin Menu Editor

http://wordpress.org/extend/plugins/admin-menu-editor/
Although the user interface team does an excellent job of developing proper navigational elements in the administrative menus, sometimes their ordering doesn't make sense. Admin Menu Editor allows a site administrator to rearrange how menus are set up, create new links to menu pages, and even limit access to some administrative pages by role.

Admin Menu Editor's slick drag-and-drop system for rearranging the order of administrative menus is intuitive.

Adminimize

http://wordpress.org/extend/plugins/adminimize/

Adminimize enables the site administrator essentially to hide any elements with the administrative menus based on roles. The common elements of WordPress are included, as are plugins that have added in their own settings pages and elements. Using CSS IDs and classes, the site administrator can even hide specific pieces of text and advertisements that some plugin authors include on their settings pages.

Hiding a settings page or option with Adminimize is as simple as clicking a checkbox and saving your settings.

FOR CONTENT CREATORS

Structured forms and fields for content entry enable content creators to focus their publishing efforts on the content and not the ambiguity that arises with unfocused user interfaces. If a staff member is supposed to be writing a piece on new acquisitions for the library, the content type should be formed as such to reflect the fields necessary to relay appropriate information to readers. Such information may include a material title, author, acquisition date, short description, rating, and link to the material in the online public access catalog (OPAC). Fields for this type of data entry are not inherent parts of WordPress page and post content types, so they require some additional tweaking to the system by way of plugins such as those listed below, or custom programming if preferred.

The More Types, More Fields, and More Taxonomies plugins described here are written by the same crew of developers, have intuitive interfaces similar in style to built-in WordPress options, and take advantage of the new custom post type, custom fields, and custom taxonomies features in the 3.0 release of WordPress.

More Types

http://wordpress.org/extend/plugins/more-types/
As its name suggests, More Types allows for the creation of new post types. By default, WordPress includes five major post types: post, page, attachment, revisions, and navigation menus. This is quite a limited selection, but More Types changes this restriction to nearly innumerable amounts. More Types enables library staff to create custom post types like staff directories, database and resource lists, and specially structured featured posts.

Part of the options screen for creation of new custom post types in More Types.

More Fields

http://wordpress.org/extend/plugins/more-fields/
The key to extending custom post types is in how the data entry is structured. Fields, or data entry points, help to focus content creation. More Fields provides fourteen different fields for data entry: single-line text box, multiline text box, what-you-see-is-what-you-get (WYSIWYG) text box, select lists, radio button lists, checkboxes, file lists, color picker, number ranges, number picker, time picker, month picker, week picker, and date picker.

The field options for More Fields.

More Taxonomies

http://wordpress.org/extend/plugins/more-taxonomies/
WordPress uses tag and category taxonomies for its posts and links manager. And though those taxonomies may work just fine for those types of content, they may not be as tailored to the specific custom post types you create. More Taxonomies allows you to create any number of custom tag- or category-based taxonomies for your custom post types.

The custom taxonomy "Subjects" built in More Taxonomies shown in the content editor for a database custom post type.

FOR EVENT PUBLISHING

There are many ways to create a calendar of events for your site, from a simple page with a list of events that are added and edited individually, to the embedding of a Google Calendar, to a full events calendar and registration system. Calendar plugins abound; the WordPress Plugins Directory lists more than two hundred. Some handle events as regular blog posts with special custom fields to handle dates, times, and locations. Other plugins handle events as custom content types, keeping them separate from news posts and allowing for more customization.

Here are some key activities that an events calendar plugin might provide:

- Creating a separate page that lists upcoming events
- Assigning categories such as Children, Teens, Adults, Book Clubs to events
- Providing a sidebar widget with a limited number of upcoming events that can be displayed on all pages and posts
- Publishing upcoming events in your news posts before the event

With these in mind, here are a few options to consider:

Google Calendar

http://www.google.com/calendar
Google's free calendar service is a popular and easy-to-use option for an events calendar. Making your Google Calendar public allows other people and organizations to add all the library's events to their own personal Google Calendar. The library's public calendar can also be easily embedded on other websites using the iframe embed code provided on the calendar's settings page. To display the calendar on the library's WordPress site, simply create a page called Events and use the embed code to display your calendar. The Google Calendar won't look neatly integrated into the page, but it should display adequately.

Kalendas

http://wordpress.org/extend/plugins/kalendas/
If you use Google Calendar for your library's events calendar, Kalendas provides a simple and nicely formatted method for displaying events on the sidebar. A list of events can also be added to any page or post using a shortcode. Clicking on an event title provides detailed event information in a nicely formatted pop-up window. This includes all the information from the event description in Google Calendar, including links and maps. Settings include date formatting options and the ability to set the maximum number of events to be displayed.

The Events Calendar

http://wordpress.org/extend/plugins/the-events-calendar/
This plugin handles events as posts with custom fields to handle dates, times, and locations. Posts are displayed in your news stream when they are published and can be automatically reposted on the day of the event. By default, posts are assigned to the category "Events," and the page http://yousite.com/category/events displays the calendar or list of events. Check the plugin's documentation and forum for tips on how to change the category used for events.

Custom templates are included for a calendar view, a list view, and a single-event view. You can choose the calendar view or list view as your site's default, yet customers can easily switch views if they like. These templates can also be customized. Additional features include options to show a Google map for event locations, a sidebar widget to display upcoming events, and integration with EventBrite (http://eventbrite.com) for handling registration.

Event Espresso

http://wordpress.org/extend/plugins/advanced-events-registration/
This robust events registration system integrates PayPal to accept fees for paid events and also handles registration for free events. The "Lite" version is free but can be used only for one event at a time. Use it to test out the basic features before you decide to upgrade to the pay-for Basic edition. This version includes a calendar with multiple display formats, online and manual registration options, built-in reCAPTCHA to combat spam, and many more features.

Safe, Sound, Tracked

SECURITY

It's a no-brainer that you need to keep your WordPress site secure, your database backed up, and your site optimized for speedy response times. Someone guessing your login and password can fill your site with spam in no time. Hackers can slip code into your files that creates tons of hidden links in your post. A failed server and your database of content could be gone. Don't let any of this happen to you. In this chapter we review tips and tricks to help keep your site in good health.

Run the Latest Version of WordPress

Make sure you are running the latest version of WordPress. You should see a nag message at the top of your WordPress back-end dashboard if a new version is available. The automatic upgrade feature in current versions of WordPress makes it really easy to keep your core software up to date. But first make sure your files are backed up.

Manage Your User Accounts

Get rid of your site's default admin user account; it is just too easy a target for hackers. To do this, log in as admin, create a new user account, and assign administrator access to the new account. Then sign in with the new account and delete the original admin account.

Set up a separate account for writing content, one that doesn't have administrator access. This helps keep the administrator credentials a bit more hidden.

Set up individual accounts for each of your site's contributors, assigning them only the level of access they need.

Get rid of unneeded user accounts.

Add Security Keys to Your wp-config.php file

To make it harder for hackers to break into your site, make sure your wp-config.php file has the security key information that was added to WordPress with version 2.6. If your file doesn't have eight lines of code that look like the code below, use the Secret Key generating service.

```
define('AUTH_KEY', 'put your unique phrase here');
define('SECURE_AUTH_KEY', 'put your unique phrase here');
define('LOGGED_IN_KEY', 'put your unique phrase here');
define('NONCE_KEY', 'put your unique phrase here');
define('AUTH_SALT', 'put your unique phrase here');
define('SECURE_AUTH_SALT', 'put your unique phrase here');
define('LOGGED_IN_SALT', 'put your unique phrase here');
define('NONCE_SALT', 'put your unique phrase here');
```

Copy and paste them into your wp-config.php file just before the line that reads:

```
/* That's all, stop editing! Happy blogging. */
```

For more information, check the WordPress Codex.[1]

Use Themes and Plugins That Are Well Known and Reliable

Delete plugins and themes you aren't using. Even though inactive plugins don't affect the amount of time it takes to load a page for a normal visitor, for an administrator they slow down the plugin and theme select pages. Additionally, keeping inactive plugins and themes that will never be used may confuse your administrative process unless you keep copious notes on why those themes and plugins are available but inactive.

BACKUP AND MAINTENANCE

Keeping your WordPress secure not only requires following best practices in setting up your installation but should include safeguards for redundancy and protections against spam. Backing up your database and installation directory regularly can be a tedious process, but necessary. Employing a plugin for this process would be an excellent addition to your overall installation. The freely available and heavily touted WP-DBManager plugin is an excellent choice, but for more options, consider purchasing BackupBuddy.

Spam is the bane of the open web. It seems embedded in every kind of website and application that allows comments and other user-created content. CMSs of all kinds, WordPress included, are prone to the same spam attacks. Luckily, WordPress has two excellent allies to rely on in the war against spam: Akismet and WP-reCAPTCHA.

WP-DBManager

http://wordpress.org/extend/plugins/wp-dbmanager/
This plugin backs up all your data tables in your WordPress database. You can run a backup on demand or schedule backups to run on a regular basis and have the backup files e-mailed to you. If in doubt about which tables to back up, do them all. And don't forget to backup the /wp-content directory on your server too.

BackupBuddy

http://pluginbuddy.com/purchase/backupbuddy/
BackupBuddy is a handy premium plugin for backing up your complete site, including the database, plugins, themes, and other content. It also has a feature to restore your site or migrate it to a new server. Note that this is a premium plugin with a cost range of $75–$197.

Akismet

http://wordpress.org/extend/plugins/akismet/
Akismet catches comments that might be spam and stores them in the comments section of your dashboard so you can review them. Akismet comes with your default installation of WordPress and requires an API key from Word Press.com.

Many of the settings options WP-DBManager provides.

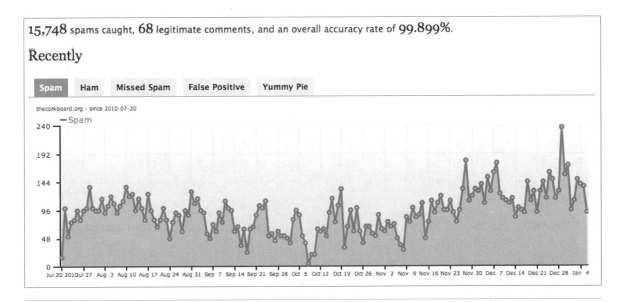

Akismet's extensive visual statistics.

WP-reCAPTCHA

http://wordpress.org/extend/plugins/wp-recaptcha/
WP-reCAPTCHA employs the often-used reCAPTCHA service to stop spam. Users inputting content on your site have to fill in a word or two of digitized text from books, text that has been turned into an image and is unreadable by spam bots.

A sample reCAPTCHA comment form enabled by WP-reCAPTCHA.

ANALYTICS

Tracking the popularity, success, and failure of your content is a necessary part of content management. By doing so, you become more knowledgeable about what is working with your content and what can be improved upon. Although analytics on content is most often done in a powerful application like Google Analytics, traveling back and forth between your website and Google Analytics' own could get a bit tiresome. Including statistical information straight into the administrative areas of WordPress would be preferred, and, luckily, three plugins—WP Stats, Analytics360, and Google Analytics Dashboard—provide just that function.

WP Stats

http://wordpress.org/extend/plugins/stats/
This plugin provides basic statistics for your site. It tracks page views, referring sites, keywords used to find your site, and what links people click on to leave your site. Like Akismet, it requires an API key from WordPress.com.[2]

Analytics360

http://wordpress.org/extend/plugins/analytics360/
Providing the power of Google Analytics with the simplified administrative user interface of
WordPress, Analytics360, built by the popular e-mail marketing company MailChimp, is an
amazing and enjoyable tool for tracking site analytics. Use the simple MailChimp settings page
to log in to your Google Analytics account and begin to see gorgeous graphs and informative
statistics indicating your popular (and not-so-popular) posts and pages.

Google Analytics Dashboard

http://wordpress.org/extend/plugins/google-analytics-dashboard/
Using the data from Google Analytics, Google Analytics Dashboard does just what its title
hints: provides statistical information in a simple-to-browse dashboard widget. Additionally,
when you visit your post and page listings, it provides quick numbers on page views, exits,
and unique visitors.

	Title	Author	Categories	Tags		Date	Analytics	
	Give those Delicious Bookmarks a WordPress Home	Kyle M.L. Jones	WordPress	Delicious, Links Manager	5	2010/12/16 Published		142 pageviews 105 exits 120 uniques

Simple stats are provided by the Google Analytics Dashboard plugin in the post listings.

NOTES

1. WordPress Codex: Editing wp-config.php, http://codex.wordpress.org/Editing_wp-config.php. For the Secret Key
   generating service, see https://api.wordpress.org/secret-key/1.1/salt/.
2. Future updates to WP Stats will be available only through the Jetpack plugin: http://wordpress.org/extend/plugins
   /jetpack/.

Flexible Design

WIDGETIZE EVERYTHING

Widgets are those boxes of content that appear on the sidebars of your site. They are useful for highlighting recent news, comments, links to other resources, customized navigation menus, contact information, and so much more. And they are not just limited to the sidebar areas. Many themes now incorporate "widget areas" in the header and footer areas, providing much more flexibility in designing your site. By default, all the pages on your site show the same widgets. But there are times when you want different widgets in different sections of your site. For example, a navigation widget on a teen-oriented page could include links to just the other teen-related pages, whereas the navigation on the main page of the site would include links to all pages on the site. The following plugins help you achieve this flexibility.

Widget Logic

http://wordpress.org/extend/plugins/widget-logic/
This plugin adds a "widget logic" field to every widget that lets you specify which pages and posts that widget should appear on. The plugin uses conditional tags such as is_home() and is_page('42')) to specify where each widget should appear. For more on conditional tags, see http://codex.wordpress.org/Conditional_Tags.

Widgets Reloaded

http://wordpress.org/extend/plugins/widgets-reloaded/
This plugin adds a myriad of flexible display options to the basic WordPress widgets through an easy-to-use interface. Each widget can also be used multiple times with different settings. Widgets Reloaded replaces these standard widgets: Archives, Authors, Bookmarks (Links), Calendar, Categories, Navigation Menu, Pages, Search, Tags.

Shiba Custom Widgets

http://shibashake.com/wordpress-theme/wordpress-custom-widgets-plugin
This plugin lets you create groups of widgets that are displayed on different pages and posts. Using the Widget Set control panel, select the widgets you want to appear together on a particular page, post, or group of pages. To assign a set to a particular page (or post), return to the edit panel for the selected page, where you see a new Shiba Widget meta-box. Select the widget set that is to appear on that page. Child pages can inherit a widget set from a parent page if you select that option in the Widget Set > Options panel.

Note that Shiba Custom Widgets is not accessible in the WordPress plugin repository. Therefore, you should exercise caution regarding the security of the plugin and the date of its most recent update.

Text Widget

Don't overlook the incredible flexibility provided by the basic text widget included in WordPress. It can contain text and HTML. Is there a message you want to have appear in a widget area of your site? Use the text widget to display it. Unfortunately, there is no WYSIWYG editor for the text widget. If you are an HTML maven, you can type your own HTML code to format the text. If not, just open a blank post and format your content there. When you are done, switch to the HTML tab, copy the code, and paste it back into the text widget.

The text widget can also be used to display content from other web services. The embed codes provided by other sites can be pasted into the text widget. This is a simple way to display a list of your recent Twitter posts, a widget for your Facebook page, a Flickr badge with your latest photos, or books posted to your GoodReads or LibraryThing account.

Enhancing the User Experience

COMMUNITY ENGAGEMENT

One of the key advantages of a WordPress site is the ease with which you can encourage communication and conversation between customers and staff, solicit feedback, and help patrons engage with staff, library content, and each other. All of this is made possible through standard WordPress functions, easy integration of third-party content, and a myriad of plugins to expand WordPress functionality.

Turn On Comments

The simplest way to get feedback from your customers is to ask them for it. So turn on the commenting feature for news posts and ask for opinions. Comments are posted immediately unless you choose to review them before they appear on your site.

The important settings for comments are found on the dashboard under Settings > Discussion (see chapter 2). Options include leaving comments open without review, letting comments from people who have already been approved post automatically, and holding all comments for review by an administrator. Make sure you turn on the option to have an e-mail sent to you when comments are received. This way you can approve comments and respond quickly.

Advertise Your Feeds

RSS feeds are built right into WordPress, but it takes a bit of searching to find them and really put them to use for your site. Peruse the WordPress Codex page to find all the RSS feeds you need, use the template tags to include them in the header of your template, or take the URLs and advertise them on your site.[1]

Social Media

Your customers are your best spokespersons, so make it easy for them to share your news, events, and other content on Facebook, Twitter, and other social sites.

Facebook Like Button

http://wordpress.org/extend/plugins/facebook-like-button/
Adding the Like button lets your readers share your content on their own Facebook page simply by clicking on it. Two options for installing:

1. There are dozens of plugins that can do this for you. The Facebook Like Button plugin is one that works well and provides several customization options.

2. If you don't mind fiddling with editing the template files (it's really not that hard), you can simply paste several lines of code into your single.php template. There is a post on wpbeginner.com that provides all the details.[2]

ShareThis

http://wordpress.org/extend/plugins/share-this/
Provide your readers with a quick way to share your content with their social networks. Select from more than fifty social networks to display on your posts in a variety of display styles. In addition to the icons you select, the ShareThis icon gives readers access to several dozen additional options. Usage statistics are available on the ShareThis.com site.

Share and Follow

http://wordpress.org/extend/plugins/share-and-follow/
This one plugin includes everything you need to make it easy for your readers to share your content. It includes a Facebook Like button, customized Twitter messages, a social network icon bar, and more. Access to a variety of specialized icon sets is available for under $15 a year.

WP to Twitter

http://wordpress.org/extend/plugins/wp-to-twitter/
With more than 370,000 downloads from the WordPress plugin repository, you can count on WP to Twitter to do all the heavy lifting in getting the published content from your site to the Twittersphere. WP to Twitter has extensive settings for customizing the message that will be published at Twitter, the ability to shorten links with a Bit.ly account, and specific analytics tracking with Google Analytics.

Polls and Surveys

Polls are a great way to get feedback from your customers and to have a bit of fun. Consider these easy-to-implement options for adding polls to your WordPress site.

PollDaddy

http://polldaddy.com/ and *http://wordpress.org/extend/plugins/polldaddy/*
This popular polling service has a plugin that allows you to create and add polls to posts and pages. It includes an easy-to-use interface for customizing the design of your poll.

WP-Polls

http://wordpress.org/extend/plugins/wp-polls/
Add and manage polls directly from the WordPress dashboard. This plugin includes a sidebar widget for putting polls on the side of all pages. The interface for customizing the design of the polls has many options but isn't as easy to use as PollDaddy.

Google Docs

https://docs.google.com/
Surveys created using Google Docs can be embedded in posts and pages. First, create a form in Google Docs, then use the embedding code provided by Google Docs to place the form on a post or page. Information gathered is stored in a Google Docs spreadsheet. This is a great way to gather suggestions, ideas, and opinions from your users.

SLICK MULTIMEDIA

Want to add an eye-catching photo gallery or slideshow to your site? Embed a video created by your teens? Add a podcast series highlighting upcoming events? Embed fun games? On its own, WordPress handles media quite nicely, but with the addition of a few plugins WordPress can be a multimedia powerhouse.

Embedding Third-Party Content

Embedding videos from YouTube, Vimeo, blip.tv, and several other sites is powered by the oEmbed protocol accomplished by simply entering the URL for the video on its own line in a post or on a page.[3] Be sure to turn this option on in Settings > Media > Auto-embeds. For example:

```
Check out this great video:
http://www.youtube.com/watch?v=-dm_x6EGIHk
```

Embedding other third-party content such as slideshows from Flickr, presentations from SlideShare, or games from other websites is simply a matter of copying the embed code from the other site and pasting it into the HTML view in your post editing box.

NextGEN Gallery

http://wordpress.org/extend/plugins/nextgen-gallery/
This flexible plugin gets better with every new version. Upload images from your computer and organize them into galleries to display in a variety of attractive formats. Additional features include editing of thumbnail images and captions.

WP-SimpleViewer

http://wordpress.org/extend/plugins/wp-simpleviewer/
This gallery plugin creates slideshows of photos in your WordPress galleries and can also pull in photos from a Flickr account.

WP jQuery Lightbox

http://wordpress.org/extend/plugins/wp-jquery-lightbox/
A Lightbox effect links thumbnails to larger images that display in an attractive overlay on the page. If there are multiple images on the page, the overlay has arrows to navigate to the next image. This effect is easily added by using one (but only one!) of the many Lightbox plugins. jQuery Lightbox is also a fine alternative.[4]

Blubrry PowerPress Podcasting Plugin

http://wordpress.org/extend/plugins/powerpress/
This full-featured podcast plugin includes support for iTunes feeds,[5] several styles of audio players, and a slew of advanced features. To post a podcast, simply write a post about the podcast and enter the full URL for your audio file in the PowerPress dialog box below the post editing box. The podcast is automatically incorporated into the post. Blubrry PowerPress Podcasting does an excellent job, but you might also consider PodPress and Podcasting Plugin by TSG.[6] Please note that audio files consume lots of server space, so carefully consider whether you will host your files on your WordPress server or on a commercial server. Location of the files doesn't affect how the plugin works.

OpenBook Book Data

http://wordpress.org/extend/plugins/openbook-book-data/
This wonderful plugin from John Miedema uses ISBNs to retrieve book covers and author, title, and publisher data from the Open Library (http://openlibrary.org) database and displays them in your posts, pages, and sidebars. It includes several default display formats and allows for custom formats as well. OpenURL resolver support is incorporated to link back to your library's catalog.

MOBILE PLUGINS AND APPS

The number of users accessing your library's website through mobile devices is growing and will continue to grow. We can no longer ignore the needs of these users. Fortunately, there are plugins that make it simple to offer a mobile version of your WordPress site. These work by detecting what browser and device a customer is using to access your site, then sending back an appropriate version of the site, optimized for the specific browser and device.

WPTouch

http://wordpress.org/extend/plugins/wptouch/
WPTouch provides an extremely elegant and easy-to-use mobile interface that includes a search function and straightforward comment forms. The pages you select to include in the mobile interface appear in a drop-down menu. There is also an option to select something other than the site's home page as the mobile default home page, providing an opportunity to create a special page of links and resources of interest to mobile users.

WordPress MultiSite Mobile Edition

http://wordpress.org/extend/plugins/wpms-mobile-edition/
This plugin is built to work with the Carrington Mobile theme, a tidy, easy-to-use mobile theme. The main view includes posts listed by title followed an unstructured (and a bit confusing) list of all the pages in your site. This plugin works with both single-site and MultiSite installations.

Apps for Your Mobile Devices

Managing your WordPress site on the go has gotten easier with apps for a variety of mobile devices. Functionality varies by device, but they all allow you to write new posts and manage comments. Other features to look for are access to statistics and the ability to delete posts and pages, upload media, turn on comment notification, and more. Watch for new features as the apps are updated. Also check to see if there are other third-party apps available for your device that might have better features.

Devices currently supported include Android, Apple (iPhone, iPad, iPod touch), Blackberry, Nokia, and Windows 7.[7]

FORMS

Forms may not be the most exciting part of a website, but they are workhorses. Forms can be used to get feedback from visitors to your site, to provide a way for patrons to order materials or ask reference questions, to offer book community rooms, and much more. These are our pick of the best forms management plugins:

Contact Form 7

http://wordpress.org/extend/plugins/contact-form-7/
This one is free, simple to use, and flexible. Create multiple forms with a full range of input field types. Fields can be required or not. It incorporates legible CAPTCHAs, quiz-type questions, and file upload options. This plugin offers full control over error and confirmation messages and formatting of resulting e-mail messages. It does all of this without an overwhelming interface.

Gravity Forms

http://www.gravityforms.com/
If you need a bit more power behind your forms, this popular and reasonably priced plugin offers a wide array of advanced options. It creates forms that display specified fields only under certain conditions, incorporates reCAPTCHAs, sets up rules to route form input to different e-mail addresses, schedules forms, and more.

Google Forms

http://docs.google.com/support/bin/topic.py?topic = 15166
Though not a plugin, this is a simple, yet effective, option for gathering information from users of your site. Set up a form using Google Docs and embed it on your WordPress page. Results are stored in a Google Docs spreadsheet for you to analyze further.

NOTES

1. "WordPress Feeds," http://codex.wordpress.org/WordPress_Feeds.
2. "How to Add Facebook Like Button in WordPress: http://www.wpbeginner.com/wp-tutorials/how-to-add-facebook-like-button-in-wordpress/.
3. For a full list of services that can be embedded with this method, see http://codex.wordpress.org/Embeds.
4. jQuery Lightbox: http://wordpress.org/extend/plugins/jquery-lightbox-balupton-edition/.
5. For more information on adding your podcast feed to iTunes, refer to "FAQs: For Podcast Makers," http://www.apple.com/itunes/podcasts/creatorfaq.html.
6. PodPress: http://wordpress.org/extend/plugins/podpress/. Podcasting Plugin by TSG: http://wordpress.org/extend/plugins/podcasting/.
7. "Apps for WordPress.com," http://en.support.wordpress.com/apps/.

Roll Your Own Social Network

TRANSFORMING WORDPRESS WITH BUDDYPRESS

Easily one of the most transformative plugins of WordPress, BuddyPress completely changes the user experience of a WordPress site by installing what is essentially a suite of social elements in one comprehensive plugin. Built originally in 2008 with its first stable version released in 2009, BuddyPress mimics some of the best qualities of Facebook but gives the site administrator the opportunity to pick and choose which elements, exactly, should be enabled. BuddyPress is also one of the most sought after plugins, with over 430,000 downloads as of January 2011.

Billed as "social networking in a box," BuddyPress enables excellent social features:

- Activity streams that consistently update with the latest blog posts, comments, forum replies, and much more
- Customizable profiles for individualizing user information
- Connection building with fellow users by way of a friending feature
- Private messaging for internal site communications between members
- Groups with stratified privacy settings
- Many more features available through some three hundred plugins created just to extend BuddyPress functionality

Like WordPress, BuddyPress is flexible for the project in which it is employed. Whereas some site creators have used BuddyPress for commercial endeavors, others like Michael Stephens and Kenley Neufeld (see their guest piece in this publication) have used it as a learning management system. One of the most successful educationally related Buddy-Press projects is the City University of New York's (CUNY) Academic Commons (http://

commons.gc.cuny.edu), which boasts over 1,500 members, 175 groups, and 300 blogs, all connecting faculty members in their intellectual pursuits at the university.

BuddyPress is supported by a team of developers who consistently update the plugin, add functionality, and are dedicated to its success. Some plugins in the WordPress plugin repository cannot boast this amount of stability, so it is excellent to be able to note that one of the most feature-heavy plugins has real staying power and can truly be relied on for a project.

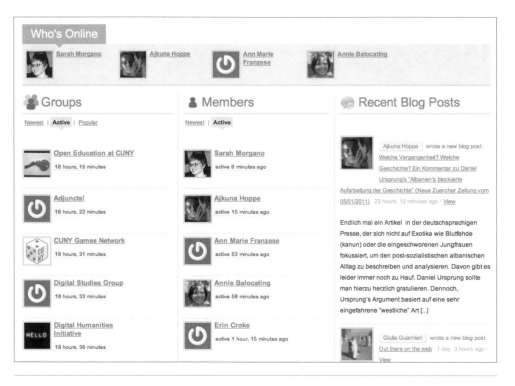

The front page of CUNY's Academic Commons shows off the most recent activity on the site.

BuddyPress

http://wordpress.org/extend/plugins/buddypress/
If a library is looking to implement social features into its site and transform it into a community-driven online location, BuddyPress should be the plugin of choice. Its features are not bested by any other plugin or combination of plugins available. The extensiveness of the plugin features does strain small servers or shared server environments. It would be best to test out BuddyPress for its scalability for particular projects. Additionally, not all themes are created with BuddyPress in mind, and therefore not all can support BuddyPress. To include BuddyPress into a theme, we suggest using the BuddyPress Template Pack plugin (see below) or choosing a BuddyPress-ready theme.

In the same fashion that plugins add features into and build functionality on top of WordPress, other plugins are created specifically to do the same for BuddyPress. As a social networking platform, the BuddyPress and WordPress connection works extremely well as is. But as users got accustomed to the general setup, they found weaknesses where greater functionality and usability could be added in. Over the past three years of BuddyPress's existence, plugin developers have recognized this and have created plugins specifically for BuddyPress.

It is difficult to sum up the following plugins in a nice, concise paragraph, for there isn't much continuity between them. That difficulty is simply representative of the disparate ways plugin developers are approaching adding functionality to BuddyPress-specific plugins.

BuddyPress Like

http://wordpress.org/extend/plugins/buddypress-like/
As the title suggests, BuddyPress Like adds in the common "Like" feature found primarily in Facebook that has also become prevalent on many sites on the Internet.

BuddyPress Links

http://wordpress.org/extend/plugins/buddypress-links/
With BuddyPress Links you can create resource lists of links on individual user profiles and within groups. It allows you to organize the link, provide descriptions, and attach an image with the link.

BuddyStream

http://wordpress.org/extend/plugins/buddystream/
Although BuddyPress creates its own activity stream of user-created content, BuddyStream enhances it by importing user content created at other social sites like Facebook, Twitter, YouTube, Flickr, and Last.fm.

BuddyPress Album+

http://wordpress.org/extend/plugins/bp-album/
BuddyPress Album+ allows users and group members to create photo albums. Future versions will include the ability to embed videos, images, and audio from popular media sites.

Group Documents

http://wordpress.org/extend/plugins/buddypress-group-documents/
Group Documents highly improves the group user experience by allowing attachments to specific groups. This plugin would be an excellent addition for sites using BuddyPress as an intranet.

Document List

Viewing item 1 to 2 (of 2 items)

Course Syllabus   Uploaded by Kyle ML Jones on 12/12/2010
The downloadable PDF of the course syllabus.
Edit | Delete

Course Schedule   Uploaded by Kyle ML Jones on 12/12/2010
The downloadable PDF of the course schedule.
Edit | Delete

Upload a New Document

A Group Documents listing.

Welcome Pack

http://wordpress.org/extend/plugins/welcome-pack/
Built by Paul Gibbs, one of the core developers of BuddyPress, Welcome Pack highly improves the user experience at the creation of a user account. As an account is created, the user can be sent welcome messages, friendship requests, and group invitations. Site administrators can use Welcome Pack to customize generic messages sent out by BuddyPress to create a more appropriate and welcoming tone in the text.

Achievements for BuddyPress

http://wordpress.org/extend/plugins/achievements/
Another fine plugin by Paul Gibbs, Achievements for BuddyPress was motivated by video game achievements found in Xbox and PlayStation3 gaming systems. Gibbs's version provides users with points and badges as they publish content and interact with a BuddyPress-enabled site.

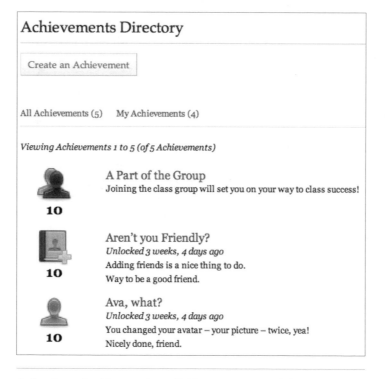

A directory of achievements available on a course website.

BuddyPress Wiki Component

http://wordpress.org/extend/plugins/bp-wiki/
Still in its infancy yet showing a lot of potential, BuddyPress Wiki Component creates simple wiki pages in groups. Page creation can be limited to just the group administrator or open to all group members. This is another excellent plugin to consider for an intranet use of BuddyPress.

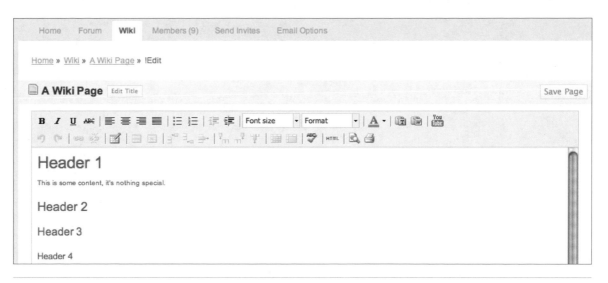

BuddyPress Wiki Component is simple to edit and use in a BuddyPress group.

BuddyPress Template Pack

http://wordpress.org/extend/plugins/bp-template-pack/
BuddyPress does not work on installation without appropriate integration into a theme. If a theme isn't BuddyPress-ready—which would be the case for a custom library theme—consider using BuddyPress Template Pack, which adds the necessary functionality for BuddyPress to work in a theme. This plugin requires a little customization to a theme even on installation, but it does not require knowledge of PHP to get it to work.

oEmbed for BuddyPress

http://wordpress.org/extend/plugins/oembed-for-buddypress/
The oEmbed plugin is a protocol for site A (such as your blog) to ask site B (such as YouTube) for the HTML needed to embed content (such as a video) from site B, and it is an automatic feature for WordPress. It is not, however, automatically enabled for BuddyPress-specific components like posting an update or in a forum topic. oEmbed for BuddyPress enables this feature for those components and enables simple embedding from these sites: YouTube, Blip .tv, Vimeo, Daily Motion, Flickr, Hulu, Viddler, Qik, Revision3, Photobucket, Scribd, and WordPress.tv.

Part IV
Guest Pieces

Creating Dynamic Subject Guides

Laura Slavin and Joshua Dodson

Laura Slavin and Joshua Dodson walk through using WordPress custom post types for subject guides at the Lincoln Memorial University Carnegie-Vincent Library.

Like most academic libraries, Carnegie-Vincent Library (CVL) built web pages from the ground up. Over the years it became apparent that the current form and design of these pages did not meet the needs of the students, faculty, staff, and community at large. The format and design of the website had become antiquated. Library staff spent hours revising the pages, often repeating the same changes on page after page. The users of the pages were inundated with a huge amount of information with poor navigational options.

The librarians at CVL were just beginning to embrace the concept of Web 2.0. They wanted the opportunity to be more involved with the website users by collaborating with students when helping them with a research question or information literacy. The other requirement was that a dynamic subject guide be created so that duplication of entry was eliminated. This also would allow librarians to provide subject expertise via the web.

How did we begin? The first step was to convince university administration that WordPress is a good solution for the library's web design needs. This was not a hard sell. Administration was pleased with our demonstrations and appreciated the fact that most of the work would be in the library with little help needed from our information services department. Soon we were beginning the famous five-minute install.

The installation was successful thanks to the expertise of our technical services technician, Joshua Dodson. A web committee was formed and training sessions were held for all librarians and staff. WordPress proved to be all that we anticipated and more.

The most innovative creation of our technical services technician was the dynamic subject guides. Joshua was able to take the custom post type functionality of WordPress and create a dynamic component that updated our ability to add and control content in our WordPress installation. Over the previous two years, WordPress had enhanced its capabilities, making it easier to provide this type of functionality. Here we offer a step-by-step guide for creating dynamic subject guides using the latest enhancements in WordPress—our most innovative WordPress endeavor at CVL.

A SUBJECT GUIDE IN WORDPRESS

It is easy to create a subject guide using WordPress, especially with the new custom post types in the WordPress core.

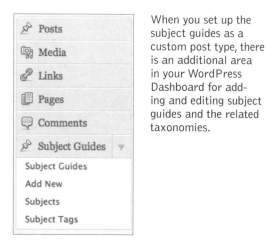

When you set up the subject guides as a custom post type, there is an additional area in your WordPress Dashboard for adding and editing subject guides and the related taxonomies.

Use the Subject Guides screen to make modifications to the subject guide posts you create.

As you add a new subject guide, treat each one as a post that is categorized within at least one subject. Your full subject guides are actually displayed by subject when utilizing the full potential of this system. It is best to add a title, a description within the post body area, the website address or linked Internet resource under the Subject Guide Options screen, the subject categories and subcategories that this post will fall under, and the appropriate subject tags. The subject categories are hierarchical, so most likely you need select only one of the subcategories per parent category.

Adding or editing the subject categories is similar to adding or editing the normal WordPress post categories. The description added here is displayed in the subject guide template.

Subject tags are similar to standard WordPress post tags. Add or modify tags by clicking Subject Tags on the left side of the WordPress Dashboard under Subject Guides.

Be sure to plan out the structure of your hierarchy before you begin creating the subject guides. You save yourself much time later on if you plan first. Also, the subject tags are much less structured and can provide additional places to describe the content in a way that does not interfere with the hierarchy you designate. The tags are a good place to add all of the extra metadata for which there is no obvious place.

A-Z Subject List

Posted on October 10, 2010 by joshua

This is the A-Z list of subjects in our subject guide.

- Subjects
  - English
  - History
  - Multidisciplinary
  - Philosophy

The A-Z Subject List displays all of the parent categories created for the subject guides. When you click on the parent category, the subcategories are listed with the descriptions and posts under them.

- Academic Search Premier - http://www.academic.search.premier.com
- America History and Life - http://www.ebsco.com
- English Example - http://www.google.com
- JSTOR - http://www.jstor.whatever
- Nihilism - http://www.iep.utm.edu/nihilism/
- Philosophy Database 1 - http://www.google.com
- Philosophy DB 2 - http://www.google.com
- Philosophy Description - http://www.google.com
- Philosophy link 1 - http://www.google.com

The Subject Guide Index lists all of the posts created as a subject guide. It lists all posts, regardless of category. Click on an individual post to go to the page for that item, which includes a description of the item and also the full list of categories and tags assigned to it.

Philosophy Database 1

Posted on October 9, 2010 by joshua

Philosophy database description 1

- Subjects: Existentialism, Realism
- Subject Tags: Database, Philosophy

An example subject guide post's individual listing.

When brought together, the complete subject guide reveals the following functionality, which includes the page title, category descriptions, subcategories, and each post that has been added beneath each subcategory. Note that this example uses simple theming options based on the WordPress default Twenty Ten theme. You can include additional customizations as you see fit by using CSS and JavaScript and by modifying the PHP and (X)HTML described below.

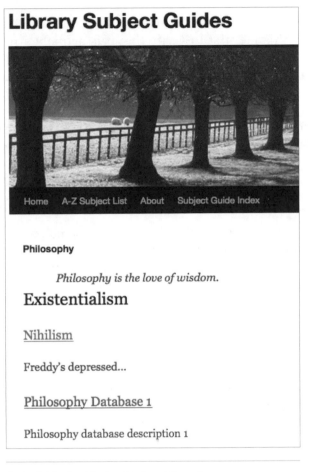

An individual subject guide for philosophy.

USING CUSTOM POST TYPES TO CREATE DYNAMIC SUBJECT GUIDES IN WORDPRESS

To preserve functionality and maintain compatibility with the current WordPress theme, we begin by creating a child theme. The newest default theme at the time of this writing is the HTML5-compatible and flexible Twenty Ten theme. We use this as our base and create a child theme so that we can take advantage of its rich structure and syntax. Creating child themes has never been easier.

First create a folder called "sg-theme" (or name it anything else you would like) and a style.css file within the folder. The only requirement is that the style sheet contain the following lines:

```
/*
Theme Name: Subject Guide 2010
Theme URI:
Description: Subject Guide 2010 Child Theme
Author: Joshua Dodson and Laura Slavin
Author URI:
Template: twentyten
Version: 1.0
*/
```

WordPress looks for this file first to verify that it is actually a regular theme or a child theme. Since we used the "Template: twentyten" declaration, WordPress now knows that we are going to inherit the functionality of the Twenty Ten theme but add some pieces to it ourselves. Note that it is important that both this folder and the original Twenty Ten folder reside in your themes folder within the wp-content folder.

At this point it is not necessary to add anything else to the style sheet, but since we want to maintain the look and feel of the original theme for our example we add the style import declaration below:

```
@import url('../twentyten/style.css');
```

To provide the full functionality of a dynamic subject guide through the use of the new WordPress custom post types, we need to add a few additional files to our new theme folder sg-theme. We add five additional files to the themes folder and one file to the plugins folder found inside of the wp-content folder.

WRITING THE PLUGIN

Let's start with the plugin that will enable the custom post types and provide the core functionality. Note that the opening lines (Plugin Name, etc.) are what WordPress automatically looks for to determine if the file is a plugin file or not.

```
<?php
/*
Plugin Name: Subject Guide Plugin
Plugin URI:
Description: Subject Guide Custom Post Types for WordPress 3.0 and above.
Author: Joshua Dodson and Laura Slavin
Version: 1.0
Author URI: http://betterwebstrategy.net
*/
class subject_guide10 {
  var $meta_fields = array('sg10-website-address');
  function subject_guide10()
  {
/*
```

The following code registers our subject guide custom post types and defines all of the variations of the term that we specify, namely "Subject Guide":

```
*/
    register_post_type('subject_guide', array(
      'labels' => array(
```

```
        'name' => __( 'Subject Guides' ),
      'singular_name' => __( 'Subject Guide' ),
      'add_new' => __( 'Add New' ),
      'add_new_item' => __( 'Add New Subject Guide' ),
      'edit' => __( 'Edit' ),
      'edit_item' => __( 'Edit Subject Guide' ),
      'new_item' => __( 'New Subject Guide' ),
      'view' => __( 'View Subject Guide' ),
      'view_item' => __( 'View Subject Guide' ),
      'search_items' => __( 'Search Subject Guides' ),
      'not_found' => __( 'No Subject Guides found' ),
      'not_found_in_trash' => __( 'No Subject Guides found in Trash' ),
      'parent' => __( 'Parent Subject Guide' ),
      ),
    'singular_label' => __('Subject Guide'),
    'public' => true,
```

This designates that we use the UI in the admin panel:

```
    'show_ui' => true,
```

This specifies that it is a custom post type, not a built-in post type:

```
    '_builtin' => false,
    '_edit_link' => 'post.php?post=%d',
    'capability_type' => 'post',
    'hierarchical' => false,
```

This sets up our permalink structure:

```
    'rewrite' => array("slug" => "subject-guide"),
    'query_var' => "subject_guide",
```

This specifies the capabilities we are going to allow the subject guide to have:

```
    'supports' => array('title','author', 'editor', 'revisions')
));
add_filter("manage_edit-subject_guide_columns", array(&$this, "edit_
columns"));
add_action("manage_posts_custom_column", array(&$this, "custom_
columns"));
/*
```

The following registers our subject guide custom taxonomies. The first taxonomy registers as hierarchical categories. The second taxonomy registers in a similar fashion as tags. Both of these allow for adding the appropriate metadata to the post:

```
*/
    register_taxonomy("subject", array("subject_guide"),
    array("hierarchical" => true, "label" => "Subjects", "singular_label" =>
    "Subject", "rewrite" => true));
    register_taxonomy("subject_tag", array("subject_guide"),
    array("hierarchical" => false, "label" => "Subject Tags", "singular_
    label" => "Subject Tag", "rewrite" => true));
/*
```

Initiate the admin interface:

```
*/
    add_action("admin_init", array(&$this, "admin_init"));
    add_action("template_redirect", array(&$this, 'template_redirect'));
    add_action("wp_insert_post", array(&$this, "wp_insert_post"), 10, 2);
    }
/*
```

This designates columns for how the custom taxonomies and the description appear in the Edit Subject Guide page:

```
*/
    function edit_columns($columns)
    {
      $columns = array(
        "title" => "Subject Guide Title",
        "sg10_description" => "Description",
        "sg10_website_address" => "Website Address",
        "sg10_subjects" => "subjects",
        "sg10_subject_tags" => "Subject Tags"
      );
      return $columns;
    }
/*
```

This function specifies the content to be displayed within the columns for Edit Subject Guide that we set up in the above code:

```
*/
    function custom_columns($column)
    {
      global $post;
      switch ($column)
      {
```

This uses the excerpt of the custom post for the description:

```
        case "sg10_description":
          the_excerpt();
          break;
```

This displays the custom URL that we use to link our custom post to an Internet resource:

```
        case "sg10_website_address":
          $custom = get_post_custom();
          echo $custom["sg10-website-address"][0];
          break;
```

This uses the hierarchical metadata for the custom post type:

```
        case "sg10_subjects":
          $subjects = get_the_terms(0, "subject");
          $subjects_html = array();
          if ($subjects) {foreach ($subjects as $subject)
            array_push($subjects_html, '<a href="' . get_term_link($subject-
```

```
>slug, "subject") . '">' . $subject->name . '</a>');
        echo implode($subjects_html, ", ");}
    break;
```

This uses the subject guide tags we create:

```
    case "sg10_subject_tags":
        $subject_tags = get_the_terms(0, "subject_tag");
        $subject_tags_html = array();
        if ($subject_tags) { foreach ($subject_tags as $subject_tag)
            array_push($subject_tags_html, '<a href="' . get_term_
            link($subject_tag->slug, "subject_tag") . '">' . $subject_tag-
            >name . '</a>');
            echo implode($subject_tags_html, ", "); }
        break;
    }
  }
/*
```

The following is an optional function that creates a redirection to take place under specific conditions. This ultimately supplies our designated templates if the page the user is viewing is one of the subject guide pages. Our taxonomy-subject.php example (see below) takes the place of the last statement by using the inherent template hierarchy structure of WordPress. The following code ultimately changes the natural structure or modifies it as necessary.

```
*/
function template_redirect()
{
  global $wp;
  $custom_types = array("subject_guide");
  if (in_array($wp->query_vars["post_type"], $custom_types))
  {
    if($wp->query_vars["name"]):
      include(STYLESHEETPATH . "/single-subject-guide.php");
      die();
    else:
      include(STYLESHEETPATH . "/category-subject.php");
      die();
    endif;
  }
}
/*
```

When a post is created or updated, this function loops through all of the post data:

```
*/
  function wp_insert_post($post_id, $post = null)
  {
    if ($post->post_type == "subject_guide")
    {
      foreach ($this->meta_fields as $key)
      {
        $value = @$_POST[$key];
        if (empty($value))
        {
          delete_post_meta($post_id, $key);
          continue;
        }
/*
```

This determines whether it is an array or string and updates or adds the metadata for the post:

```
*/
        if (!is_array($value))
        {
          if (!update_post_meta($post_id, $key, $value))
          {
            add_post_meta($post_id, $key, $value);
          }
        }
        else
        {
          delete_post_meta($post_id, $key);
          foreach ($value as $entry)
            add_post_meta($post_id, $key, $entry);
        }
      }
    }
  }
  /*
```

This function allows us to create custom metaboxes for the Edit Subject Guide page:

```
*/
  function admin_init()
  {
    add_meta_box("sg10-meta", "Subject Guide Options", array(&$this, "meta_
    options"), "subject_guide", "normal", "high");
  }
  /*
```

This function specifies the content and display for our subject guide in the admin screen:

```
*/
  function meta_options()
  {
    global $post;
    $custom = get_post_custom($post->ID);
    $website_address = $custom["sg10-website-address"][0];
?>
<p>
  <label>Website Address:</label>
  <br />
  <input name="sg10-website-address" value="<?php echo $website_address; ?>"
/>
</p>
<?php
  }
}
/*
```

Now we have finished setting up how WordPress handles all of our subject guide custom post types and the metadata and other taxonomies associated with it. All that is left to do is to initiate the plugin, which is taken care of in the following lines:

```
*/
add_action("init", "subject_guide10Init");
function subject_guide10Init() { global $sg10; $sg10 = new subject_
guide10(); }
?>
```

CREATING THE TEMPLATES

The plugin does most of the heavy lifting for us on the admin side. Now we need to specify how we are going to display the contents of our subject guide custom posts. We handle this through our templates. Since we are using a child theme, WordPress looks at our custom folder first and displays the content we specify for our templates. After it looks at our child theme folder, WordPress looks for the rest of the functionality in the parent theme folder.

Subject Guide Taxonomy Template

Using the built-in WordPress theme structure, we create a file called taxonomy-subject.php. We use the categorization to display the subjects, so that when one clicks on the category all of the posts classified as that subject and all of the subcategories with their respective posts are displayed in a hierarchical fashion.

Note that there is a lot going on in this example. This is really the bread and butter of the subject guide system in terms of the way it is displayed. This example does most of the heavy lifting for us.

```
<?php
/*
```

The taxonomy-subject.php file takes advantage of the internal taxonomy template system of WordPress. Since our custom taxonomy is "subject," WordPress looks at the taxonomy -[custom taxonomy name here].php file structure and uses this file for the look and feel of our first-level subject categories.

We start by setting the variables and getting the header:

```
$term = get_term_by( 'slug', get_query_var( 'term' ), get_query_var(
'taxonomy' ) );
$tax = get_query_var( 'taxonomy' );
get_header(); ?>
<div id="container">
  <div id="content" role="main">
    <h1 class="page-title"><?php echo $term->name; ?></h1>
    <?php if ($term->description) { ?>
    <blockquote><?php echo $term->description; ?></blockquote>
    <?php } ?>
    <?php
/*
```

If there are subcategories, retrieve them and display them as a Heading 2 and also display the description of the category.

```
*/
        if (get_term_children($term->term_id, $tax) != null) {
```

```
              $term_children = get_terms(
                $tax,
                array(
                  'child_of' => $term->term_id,
                )
              );
              foreach ($term_children as $term_child) {
                echo '<h2>' . $term_child->name . '</h2>';
                if ($term_child->description) { ?>
  <blockquote><?php echo $term_child->description; ?></blockquote>
  <?php }
              query_posts(array(
                'subject' => $term_child->slug,
                'orderby' => 'title',
                'order' => 'ASC',
                )
              );
      /*
```

The following code looks through all of the posts categorized with the subcategory and displays the title of the post as a link to the subject URL (*not* the permalink to the post), and it also displays the content of the post. This allows any additional information, links, or images of the post to be displayed.

```
      */
              if (have_posts()) : ?>
    <?php while (have_posts()) : the_post(); ?>
    <h3 <?php post_class(); ?>>
      <?php global $post;
              $custom = get_post_custom($post->ID);
              $website_address = $custom["sg10-website-address"][0];
              ?>
      <a href="<?php if($website_address) { echo $website_address; } else {
      the_permalink(); } ?>">
      <?php the_title(); ?>
      </a> </h3>
    <?php the_content(); ?>
    <?php endwhile; ?>
    <?php endif;
              }
      /*
```

If there are no subcategories, only the post titles for the top-level custom taxonomy are displayed.

```
      */
            } else {
              if (have_posts()) : ?>
    <ul>
      <?php while (have_posts()) : the_post(); ?>
      <li <?php post_class(); ?>> <a href="<?php the_permalink(); ?>">
        <?php the_title(); ?>
        </a> </li>
      <?php endwhile; ?>
    </ul>
    <?php endif;
            }
```

```
          ?>
    </div>
    <!-- #content -->
</div>
<!-- #container -->
<?php get_sidebar(); ?>
<?php get_footer(); ?>
```

Subject Guide Index

This template lists all of the subject guide posts across all categories (subjects) and displays the URL of the Internet resource next to it. When the post title link is clicked on, it takes you to the single page listing of the post resource.

```php
<?php
/* Template Name: Subject Guide Index */
get_header(); ?>
<div id="container">
  <div id="content" role="main">
    <ul>
      <?php
global $post;
$tmp_post = $post;
$myposts = get_posts(array(
'post_type' => 'subject_guide',
'numberposts' => -1,
'orderby' => 'title',
'order' => 'ASC',
));
  foreach($myposts as $post) :
    setup_postdata($post);
  ?>
      <?php global $post;
          $custom = get_post_custom($post->ID);
          $website_address = $custom["sg10-website-address"][0];
          ?>
        <li><a href="<?php the_permalink() ?>" rel="bookmark"
        title "Permanent Link to <?php the_title(); ?>">
          <?php the_title(); ?>
          </a> - <?php echo $website_address; ?></li>
        <?php endforeach; ?>
      <?php $post = $tmp_post; ?>
    </ul>
  </div>
<!-- #content -->
</div>
<!-- #container -->
<?php get_sidebar(); ?>
<?php get_footer(); ?>
```

The Subject Guide A–Z List template and the Subject Guide Category template take on basic functionality from the standard Twenty Ten loop. We use our functions.php file to make some modifications to this to provide additional functionality. Note that the Subject Guide A–Z List template takes on the page loop functionality, whereas the Subject Guide Category template uses the single post loop.

Subject Guide A–Z List

```php
<?php
/* Template Name: Subject Guide Subject A-Z List */
get_header(); ?>
  <div id="container">
    <div id="content" role="main">
      <?php get_template_part( 'loop', 'page' ); ?>
    </div><!-- #content -->
  </div><!-- #container -->
  <?php get_sidebar(); ?>
<?php get_footer(); ?>
```

Subject Guide Category

```php
<?php
/* Template Name: Subject Guide Category */
get_header(); ?>
  <div id="container">
    <div id="content" role="main">
      <?php get_template_part( 'loop', 'single' ); ?>
    </div><!-- #content -->
  </div><!-- #container -->
  <?php get_sidebar(); ?>
<?php get_footer(); ?>
```

Functions.php

To bring everything together, we use a custom functions.php file:

```php
<?php
/*
```

This function includes additional classes to the built-in body class, allowing additional styling of the subject guide posts within the CSS style sheet.

```php
*/
function taxonomy_body_class( $classes ) {
    if( is_tax() ) {
      global $taxonomy;
      if( !in_array( $taxonomy, $classes ) )
        $classes[] = "taxonomy " . "taxonomy-".$taxonomy;
      }
    return $classes;
}
add_filter('body_class','taxonomy_body_class');
/*
```

The following two functions allow us to pull the full taxonomy list of terms that are associated with each of our subject guide posts.

```php
*/
function sg_get_terms( $id = '' ) {
  global $post;
  if ( empty( $id ) )
    $id = $post->ID;
  if ( !empty( $id ) ) {
    $post_taxonomies = array();
    $post_type = get_post_type( $id );
    $taxonomies = get_object_taxonomies( $post_type , 'names' );
    foreach ( $taxonomies as $taxonomy ) {
      $term_links = array();
      $terms = get_the_terms( $id, $taxonomy );
      if ( is_wp_error( $terms ) )
        return $terms;
      if ( $terms ) {
        foreach ( $terms as $term ) {
          $link = get_term_link( $term, $taxonomy );
          if ( is_wp_error( $link ) )
            return $link;
          $term_links[] = '<a href="' . $link . '" rel="' . $taxonomy .
          '">' . $term->name . '</a>';
        }
      }
      $term_links = apply_filters( "term_links-$taxonomy" , $term_links );
      $post_terms[$taxonomy] = $term_links;
    }
    return $post_terms;
  } else {
    return false;
  }
}
function sg_get_terms_list( $id = '' , $echo = true ) {
  global $post;
  if ( empty( $id ) )
    $id = $post->ID;
  if ( !empty( $id ) ) {
    $my_terms = sg_get_terms( $id );
    if ( $my_terms ) {
      $my_taxonomies = array();
      foreach ( $my_terms as $taxonomy => $terms ) {
        $my_taxonomy = get_taxonomy( $taxonomy );
        if ( !empty( $terms ) )
        $my_taxonomies[] = '<span class="' . $my_taxonomy->name .
        '-links">' . '<span class="entry-utility-prep entry-utility-prep-'
        . $my_taxonomy->name . '-links">' . $my_taxonomy->labels->name . ':
        ' . implode( $terms , ', ' ) . '</span></span>';
      }
      if ( !empty( $my_taxonomies ) ) {
        $output = '<ul>' . "\n";
        foreach ( $my_taxonomies as $my_taxonomy ) {
          $output .= '<li>' . $my_taxonomy . '</li>' . "\n";
        }
        $output .= '</ul>' . "\n";
      }
      if ( $echo )
        echo $output;
      else
        return $output;
    } else {
    return;
    }
```

```
  } else {
    return false;
  }
}
/*
```

This applies a filter that inserts the subject list within the Subject Guide A-Z List template:

```
*/
add_filter('the_content','insert_subject_list');
function insert_subject_list($content) {
  if ( is_page_template('subject-guide-subject-a-z.php') ) {
    echo $content;
    $args = array(
  'orderby'           => 'name',
  'order'             => 'ASC',
  'show_last_update'  => 0,
  'style'             => 'list',
  'show_count'        => 0,
  'hide_empty'        => 1,
  'use_desc_for_title'  => 1,
  'child_of'          => 0,
  'hierarchical'         => true,
  'title_li'          => __( 'Subjects' ),
  'number'            => NULL,
  'echo'         => 1,
  'depth'             => 1,
  'current_category'  => 0,
  'pad_counts'        => 0,
  'taxonomy'          => 'subject' );
  wp_list_categories( $args );
  }
  else {return $content;}
}
/*
```

Here we apply a filter that modifies the single subject guide item display to also show the full taxonomy listing for that item:

```
*/
add_filter('the_content','insert_custom_taxonomy');
function insert_custom_taxonomy($content) {
  if (is_singular('subject_guide')) {
    echo $content;
    $content.= "<div class='taxonomy'>";
    $content.= sg_get_terms_list();
    $content.= "</div>";
  }
  else {return $content;}
}
?>
```

Creating dynamic subject guides using WordPress adds a level of usability to your library website, enabling you to add and manage content with greater efficiency. As we discovered at CVL, these guides also help involve librarians and users.

Using WordPress gives CVL a professional, functional presence on the web. What is exciting about WordPress is that it is evolving and improving. No matter the size of your library or your specific needs, WordPress almost always provides a solution. With the step-by-step guide provided here, we hope you take the time to experiment with our response to a specific need at our library and then branch out and utilize the multifaceted capabilities of WordPress.

MORE INFORMATION

This is really just the tip of the iceberg. We fully expect that WordPress will release even more customizable functionality in the future. The WordPress Codex is the top resource for all things WordPress. It is best to look there first for the definitive word on how to use WordPress functions and capabilities. With that said, there are many additional resources on the web that provide tips and different approaches. WordPress is expanding into a fully functional content-management system—it has been for a while. The beauty in using and customizing a system like WordPress is that, the more people who use it, the more support is provided. The full community of support in WordPress is a remarkable thing. You never know when your question will be answered by another user who has experienced the same issues, or even one of the lead developers.

Please look at the following references and resources for more information on using Word-Press and custom post types:

- WordPress Custom Post Types on the WordPress Codex: http://codex.wordpress .org/Custom_Post_Types
- Showing custom post types on your home/blog page: http://justintadlock.com /archives/2010/02/02/showing-custom-post-types-on-your-home-blog-page
- Custom post types in WordPress: http://justintadlock.com/archives/2010/04/29 /custom-post-types-in-wordpress
- Custom post types in WordPress 3.0: http://kovshenin.com/archives/custom-post -types-in-wordpress-3-0/
- Extending Custom Post Types in WordPress 3.0: http://kovshenin.com/archives /extending-custom-post-types-in-wordpress-3-0/

As with all open source code, the core WordPress functionality may change and leave sections of the code presented here nonfunctional. If you choose to implement the ideas expressed here, please research WordPress further and share your findings with the WordPress community. We do not guarantee exact results as expressed here.

Laura Slavin is the technical services librarian at Lincoln Memorial University Carnegie-Vincent Library. She earned her MLIS from the University of South Florida School of Library and Information Science and her MBA from Lincoln Memorial University. Joshua Dodson is a web analytics strategist for Stamats, Inc., in Cedar Rapids, Iowa. Laura and Joshua have published and presented numerous times on WordPress and the use and customization of other open source software for over the past two years.

First-Year Seminar Blogs

Jacob Hill and Peg Cook

Jacob Hill and Peg Cook discuss using WordPress MultiSite blogs at the Elmhurst College A. C. Buehler Library in a program for first-year students.

We knew of WordPress as a web publishing tool long before we considered it as a teaching and learning tool. The concept of a comprehensive solution for our faculty and students needs took us a while to recognize and embrace; up until a few years ago, our demand for self-hosted server applications was relatively minor. The gap was filled by web-based applications such as Blogger and Blogspot, which seemed to work as long as class assignments didn't demand too much in the way of user flexibility or administrative control. There were some instructors who had requests for website design and publishing capability; to solve this, we offered public wikis (PBWiki and Wikispaces) and student server space for those who were familiar with some form of web-authorship coding or software (writing HTML code, using Word, Frontpage, or Dreamweaver), for which we offered limited instruction. We did have some advanced content management tools already at our fingertips (Blackboard and Moodle), but the main impediment was the basic unsuitability of these tools for assignment needs. Professors generally wanted a content publishing tool with a powerful-but-simple editing capability on the student side combined with some selective visibility or sharing mechanism and the ability to leave comments.

At the time (circa 2006/7), many librarians did not see the potential relationship between blogging and website design (or, at the very least, they did not think these mechanisms could be served by one product). We had heard of subscription-based tools that could do both, but funds weren't going to be allocated until we had significant demand. In addition, the blogging-versus-website camps had pitched their tents and started to lobby for their favorite platform. Blogging was popular and easy, and it had buzz as a "hot" publishing medium. It also had the advantage (or weakness, depending on what you wanted) of chronological content arrangement. Website content design was seen as more difficult, static, and (perhaps) harder to support; wikis, with their WYSIWYG editors, were seen as "good enough" and filled the role when needed.

Librarians tended to support this potpourri of blog and wiki tools on the basis of personal preferences and experience; it was the "if you have a hammer, everything looks like a nail" approach. Once you acquired skill in Blogger or PBWiki, you tended to offer that as the solution for faculty needs. It was not an ideal situation, but it did make sense in terms of time commitment and technical knowledge.

The idea of using a self-hosted instance of WordPress was brought to our attention by a new hire for our library technology specialist position. He had been using a personal installation for some time. A self-hosted tool was attractive since it would help us retain control of the administrative side of the product. In addition, our employee was able to demonstrate some of the advantages of WordPress for both users and viewers. Particularly, the following things caught our eye:

- Under our administrative control
- Integration with our LDAP authentication
- Easy user and account creation
- Powerful yet easy WYSIWYG or HTML editor
- Moderate learning curve
- Selective visibility (public vs. private)
- Robust and tested
- Perhaps most essential, ability to offer both static "pages" (i.e., website) and blog posts, accomplishing multiple aims at one time

IMPLEMENTING WORDPRESS FOR FIRST-YEAR SEMINAR STUDENTS

A key component of the integration of WordPress blogs and web pages into our library practice is Elmhurst College's First Year Seminar (FYS) program. First piloted in the fall of 2008, our FYS is structured around several common elements. The decision was made early on in the process of designing the FYS curriculum to integrate information technology skills and information ethics, and an assignment set was created that utilized a blogging platform, allowing students to report on their FYS activities and complete writing assignments that had a potentially wider audience than just their classroom instructor.

Originally, we chose Blogger as the platform for the initial pilot trial of the FYS assignment, partly for technical reasons and partly because of the FYS librarian's familiarity with it. However, that first year highlighted some issues with Blogger. Students had to create Google accounts, which gave them another set of user names and passwords to forget. Additionally, some students already had Google accounts, which complicated the process, and administration of the "cloud" program was impossible on a local front.

In the second year of the pilot, we decided to switch to a local installation of WordPress Multi-User (MU), now called WordPress MultiSite. The number of students involved in the FYS pilot had doubled, and we needed a more locally manageable tool with features that Blogger lacked. WordPress gave us the ability to create blogs and web pages quickly, add users in various capacities to blogs, and quickly and easily troubleshoot issues that student and faculty were having.

WordPress also gave us the opportunity to allow faculty to use the platform as a content management and communication tool within the context of their course. Some faculty took more advantage of this than others, using the blog to post assignments, links to relevant sources of information or readings, schedules, and so on. All sections used the blogging feature as a way to store links for all students' blogs in one place.

REFLECTION AND FUTURE CONSIDERATIONS

We have been using the self-hosted WordPress installation for two years. Surprisingly, not many students have been familiar with it, even though it has been publicly available for some time either as a self-hosted instance or from WordPress.com. Even more revealing was the very small number of students who had ever blogged or created websites. We had a perception of millennials as a group who were competent and prolific users of Web 2.0 tools. Our experience demonstrated that this is no more true for this age group than for any other: some people are technophiles and comfortable using different products, some are familiar and comfortable with one or two tools (Facebook and e-mail, for example), and some (even millennials) are technophobes and do not have a high comfort level with technology.

Additionally, the use of WordPress in the FYS class has changed over time as the courses and assignments evolved. The initial use of the blogs was a mandatory part of the information ethics unit, but the mandatory blog use was not feasible for many of the FYS course instructors, so we made it optional. A third of the instructors of the course this fall seem to be using the blog to one degree or another, but we also have had increased use of the platform as a website creation tool.

Our satisfaction and confidence with WordPress is evident by our decision, in the summer of 2007, to use it for creating and hosting the primary library website (http://library.elmhurst .edu). The site is primarily administrated and updated by librarians, and WordPress allows us to keep this "in-house" without resorting to more complex web editing software and direct FTP site uploads. We have been very happy with the ways in which WordPress allows us to easily post web page content; perhaps ironically, the librarians rarely use the blogging feature but instead use its web design features, which are simple yet powerful. Although we may choose to migrate to some other platform in the future, we see little lacking in WordPress and plan on using it for the foreseeable future.

Jacob Hill has served since 2003 as a reference and instruction librarian for the A. C. Buehler Library at Elmhurst College (Illinois). He has recently presented and published on plagiarism detection software, mobile resource access, and reference desk communication applications. He is currently investigating college/secondary education liaison program partnerships. Peg Cook is a reference and instruction librarian at Elmhurst College. She works closely with first-year students and is interested in the relationship between technology and information literacy. Peg has an MA in performance studies from Northwestern University as well as an MSLIS from Dominican University.

BuddyPress and Higher Education

Michael Stephens and Kenley Neufeld

Kyle Jones interviews Michael Stephens and Kenley Neufeld, two instructors using BuddyPress as a learning management system.

Online learning has become ubiquitous across most educational organizations in the United States. To support this learning environment, institutions have typically chosen to implement one or two learning management systems on campus. These large software implementations bring standardization, support, and integration into existing campus systems. For some, these standard systems don't always meet the needs of students and faculty. Both Michael Stephens and Kenley Neufeld have been experimenting with alternative tools. In this discussion we explore how these two instructors have implemented a WordPress/BuddyPress learning system for their students.

KYLE. Do you find that creating a virtual learning community is much more feasible now, with today's technical tools like WordPress, than it was several years ago?

KENLEY. We've reached a point of critical mass. The tools and software available are pretty ubiquitous. If you think about WordPress, anybody can get a WordPress site up and running even if they are not fully aware that's what they are doing. It's moved outside just the fringe and more into the mainstream. This makes it easier for people to step into it. If I use the word "WordPress" in public, some might actually know what that is, or if I just mention "blog" then they most likely will understand. Whereas a decade ago if I had said a MOO, I'd have to spend 10-minutes explaining it and even then they might not get it. Part of this has to do with the change in the Internet landscape. A decade ago it wasn't small, but the Internet has become pretty much present in everybody's lives today. Everyone seems to be engaged with it on some level. That alone is going to shift the tool mechanisms to facilitate learning environments. Blackboard was really the only player on the market a decade ago.

MICHAEL. I'm reminded of the years I spent doing tech training at the public library and then taking over the training and development department. Between 1996 and 2003, we really struggled to design an intranet—now all you need is a blog behind a firewall and you suddenly have an intranet. It amazes me how easy this stuff is now. Because the technology got easier and more popular, everyday folks now understand "we're running this on WordPress or Drupal or Blogger"—that's been one of the most exciting things about this. And this is why we should be doing these things in library school, and in the university; these are the tools of the moment. In three or four years we might be talking about something else. But the ideas and motivations remain the same.

KYLE. You both work at institutions where you have some kind of formal learning management system. Why did you make the decision to not use the resources you had? You could have made your lives extremely easier going with the norm, and instead you chose to roll your own. You put a lot of struggles on yourself to do so.

MICHAEL. I can't have my students spend so much time creating and writing inside a tool that they'll probably never touch once they graduate, unless maybe they work in academic libraries. They should be using a tool or a handful of tools they will be using in their jobs. I want them to come out of the program and say they have used WordPress and took advanced web design and experienced Drupal and used Twitter. That's much more important than these systems. The feeling that I'm serving the students better by using these systems is good.

KENLEY. For me, it's been more about trying to build tools that will meet the needs of the types of things I want incorporated. The system we had originally, WebCT, I used for only one semester and was very disappointed. As a result, I started using Moodle the following term and then the college went to Moodle as well (thankfully). I do use Moodle, and it works well for the most part, but I found it a little bit clunky here and there for some things I'm trying to accomplish.

The main reason I'm using WordPress/BuddyPress is because the class I'm teaching has to do with social media. Since the class focus is social media and social networking, it seemed like the obvious solution would be to actually use the tools that I'm teaching about. It was a non-decision. This is what we're going to use, and I've been very happy. Now, as I look ahead, and if I were to teach other classes without the heavy social media focus, then I would still be inclined toward using the WordPress/BuddyPress solution. I am comfortable with it and happy with it. But I also need to think about the overall student experience and recognize that the school does support one system, which is Moodle, and rather than have students learn a new system it may be smarter to stick with Moodle. It would really depend on the class. In the current situation, WordPress is the obvious solution.

Fortunately, learning management systems are trying to incorporate more of the social media tools where you can easily incorporate the video and the audio—the interactivity and visual representations that people seek. I haven't looked at Blackboard in a couple years, so I'm not that familiar with it, but with Moodle you can incorporate just about anything. There are methods to do it, but you are still building within a framework, though it is customizable. It will depend on the support you have locally, because most instructors are not going to go the extra step unless they have an easy mechanism in order to do so. On our campus we are working in that direction—to support instructors to add other types of media content, interactively, to allow for a richer learning environment. It is possible.

MICHAEL. I taught twenty-five students this summer using WordPress/BuddyPress doing Internet Fundamentals. What Kenley said about media is incredibly important, and this summer I would be out on the hiking trail with the dog and my iPhone. I'd be thinking about what I'd like to tell the students, so I recorded a video that isn't just a talking head. They see a tree going by, or the lake, or the dog, and they hear my voice saying they are doing really great, and here are some things to think about while doing this next exercise. And the feedback I got from the students for a three-minute video was that they loved it. It helped them feel connected and it helped me feel more connected with them. It became part of what we were doing.

KENLEY. Goes back to philosophy. The human touch.

KYLE. What about the WordPress/BuddyPress combination promotes the human touch?

MICHAEL. I request that everyone use some type of profile photo—it doesn't have to be their face—but I want to see something. The red car. The teapot. That helps me associate that image with that person, their writing, and their interaction on the site. It's amazing how far associating a little photo with someone's writing goes beyond what could be so text-based in an online class. The Twitter-like feature, what used to be called "The Wire"—it's very fluid and pleasant.

KENLEY. Definitely agree that the avatar piece builds a connection between students and between instructor and the students. We can identify easily with who this person is in the class. My class is 100% online, so this is the only mechanism I have to know students. The other element that is important is that students are working with their own blog within WordPress and can therefore create something that is uniquely themselves. They can create multiple blogs. They could create one just for the coursework or add a second one for a hobby they are working on to utilize the environment and to play. That is the type of advantage we have with this type of software.

I do like the new shift away from the BuddyPress "wire" to the "status update" model—it makes more sense. The whole aspect of the profile page in BuddyPress is something that I find very useful. When I set up the system, I have the default landing page for each person as their own profile page. They see themselves and their own activity. They see the friends they have made in the class. It builds on that concept of a community versus coming to a home page—there are elements of that on the home page but it is more structured toward the class material rather than some of the community aspects. It's not as significant on the home page.

KYLE. What about WordPress/BuddyPress doesn't work for your classroom or for your students?

KENLEY. There is the initial need to understand the framework. That will occur in just about any online learning environment. When you walk into a physical classroom, you know what to do. It's something that we're used to and we've done it for twenty to twenty-five years before we get to college. We still have this problem in the online environment where there is a period in which you're trying to familiarize yourself and get acclimatized to the online environment. That is probably the biggest challenge for students—the technological aspect of where things are and what the expectations are.

The second challenge for my students is being able to take on the same level of transparency that I'm demonstrating—to get them to let go of some of their privacy. I don't require my students to make their blogs public, though it is strongly encouraged. [*Side note:* There is a technical limitation in WordPress/BuddyPress: when students mark their blogs as private, then they don't show up in the regular blog feed for other students. I do have a couple students who have blogs marked private because they don't want Google crawling their site. Obviously, this limits the interaction their sites will have from their classmates, but I can still go and look at the blog and interact.] That is a big limitation—working with privacy/transparency aspects. In regards to the avatars, it doesn't matter to me if it's not a picture of the person, but it is important that it's something. That image represents the student in the class.

MICHAEL. I agree with both of Kenley's identified challenges. There are some nitty-gritty things too. I think it goes back to understanding the site. When the blog posts roll off the front page, then how do we find them?

One thing that really impressed me was last year there was an update mid-semester, and Kyle and I were going back and forth on whether we should update. Should we wait? We decided to put it out to the students. Do you think we should do it? I gave them a little push and they voted. It was a landslide vote to do the site update and see what happens. It went very well. Kyle and I were pretty nervous.

KYLE. I was extremely worried about that, but I'm not in charge of your class. In terms of upgrading to a major version of anything new, there is always that risk that bugs are uncovered. That could really blow up whatever you are working on. I think your students would have recognized this, but it would have been a learning experience too. If they are in their library and they are updating a piece of software, then what are the problems that could occur? Who is it going to affect? What trouble could I possibly be in?

We are in a bug culture—we use mainstream tools like Facebook and Twitter. Just this week Facebook went down for several hours and Twitter had a javascript issue. It's a buggy culture and we have to learn to get through it and find the resolution to make it better next time.

KENLEY. I couldn't have done that with my class. Every time I go to the dashboard and I see the plugin updates, I don't even want to know about that stuff. It always makes me nervous.

KYLE. That's one of the levels that students don't really see—what's going on in terms of plugins and what could happen to their class. They shouldn't have to worry about that—that's a system admin thing. But in Michael's situation, here you have him presenting them with potential opportunities and improvements to their learning experience.

KENLEY. We don't do bugs on our campus. It has to be planned and vetted. Even then we might spend six months or more discussing it. There's a shell-shocked nature on our campus because of some bad experiences in the past. A significant hesitance is present where something might potentially negatively impact (or improve) the learning environment.

KYLE. Have either of you talked to your peers about using WordPress/BuddyPress more extensively throughout different classes?

MICHAEL. I have done a couple presentations as part of our Center for Teaching and Learning Excellence. I also have a couple colleagues who have adapted similar systems.

KENLEY. I've spoken with some colleagues and spoken with our faculty support department. There are faculty using WordPress in other classroom environments. However, they are not using the BuddyPress combination. That would be a different step, requiring additional support and training. There is some interest across campus. Even though I'm just one person, we are a small campus and I communicate things that I read or experience with the dean responsible for online technologies by keeping him apprised of what I'm doing, and maybe that is something people would be interested in trying out.

KYLE. Since you've talked to your peers, maybe the word has gotten out to your systems department. Have they reached out to you to say we'd like to help you in this venture?

KENLEY. No. It's actually the opposite. They say to me, "There is somebody interested in using WordPress, can you help them?" I'm one of the people they send interested parties to. If I came to the campus support and said I'd like to host WordPress/BuddyPress on-site, they probably would consider it, but it is just simpler to keep it off-site. The other faculty using WordPress do use an on-campus installation run through our Faculty Resource Center. On the IT side of the house, as opposed to faculty resource support, they probably don't have the mechanisms or the staff to implement this on a broader scale.

KYLE. What about you, Michael?

MICHAEL. Very similar. There are pockets of people all over campus using WordPress to varying degrees. Some people are experimenting with Moodle. We're all sort of finding our way. The next step is it might become more strategic—more planned. We'll get more support as we go forward. I host off-site because it is easier.

KENLEY. Currently, I am running on a virtual private server ($50/month) because of problems with memory resource usage of BuddyPress. The hosting provider moved me to a VPS because of high memory use. As a result, I've had to reboot the server several times to resolve memory spikes.

KYLE. This is a limitation that has been discussed in the BuddyPress forums. It is very frustrating because we expect a WordPress plugin to just work and not affect your resources in that way. That is the general experience with WordPress. There is a lot of complexity built into BuddyPress because of the new features it is offering and the queries it is pulling from the database.

KENLEY. In the last day or two, the memory usage has been around 200–300 MB of memory use. But it spikes up to over 800 MB a few times a day. In a shared hosting environment this will not work.

KYLE. This could be improved in the future, but the complexity might increase at the same time. What are you planning to do differently with your course sites in the future? What is on your wishlist of features? Are you going to migrate away from WordPress? Any specific things you'd like to include?

KENLEY. I would like to include a solid grade book tool. I haven't done the research to find one, so I currently post my grades in Moodle since all classes have a shell on our campus. The second thing would be some type of LDAP [Lightweight Directory Access Protocol] authentication to bounce against our campus system. Again, I haven't spent the time to research this option, and it would require some institutional support and sign-off. I know both are possible.

MICHAEL. I see continuing using WordPress for a while; it is working very well. I would like to see better integration with some of the other social tools. Everyone got on Twitter in the emerging technologies class so I wish there was a way to mash that up a little bit better.

KENLEY. In my grading process I like to look at each student blog. I was originally using the WordPress dashboard to navigate through all the blogs but have since discovered that the front-end activity feed meets this need well. From a teacher perspective, the mechanism for working my way through the content for grading purposes, knowing who is being engaged, etc., is very important. The first semester I used WordPress/BuddyPress it seemed very time consuming. It's much better now.

MICHAEL. I really like the activity feed. I subscribe to all of the feeds from all of the sites. I had a class with twenty-five people, twenty-five blogs, ten blog posts a semester, and that's 250 blog posts. That's a lot. I don't expect the students to read everyone's post, but I do read everything. Finding ways where smaller groups might participate with each other instead of twenty-five people trying to find a blog post to comment on.

KYLE. Thank you both for your insights and for sharing your innovative spirit with the readers of this technology guide. Furthermore, thank you for rethinking the online learning experience. I imagine your students are appreciative of your hard work and development on your course sites.

Michael Stephens is an assistant professor of the School of Library and Information Science, San José (California) State University. He utilizes WordPress/BuddyPress to create interactive social learning sites for his classes. He writes the monthly column "Office Hours" in *Library Journal*, exploring issues, ideas, and emerging trends in library and information science education, and blogs at http://tametheweb.com. He speaks and researches internationally on emerging technologies, learning, and libraries. Kenley Neufeld is currently the library director at Santa Barbara (California) City College. He has been using the Internet to teach and train people since early 1993, when the first graphical web browser was created.

From LibGuides to WordPress

Paul Boger

Paul Boger explains the history, inspiration, success, and failures of using WordPress to create subject guides at the Stafford Campus Library of the University of Mary Washington.

Founded in 1908, the University of Mary Washington (UMW) has slowly grown into a two-campus institution. The original campus is located in Fredericksburg, Virginia, and the second campus, opened in 1999, is in nearby Stafford County. The students of Mary Washington have access to library services at both campuses. The Simpson Library serves the faculty, staff, and students at the main campus in Fredericksburg, and the Stafford Campus Library serves the faculty, staff, and students at the Stafford location. The Stafford Campus Library, though with a small degree of autonomy, operates as a branch of the Simpson Library. Although there are many similarities in resources, collections, and policies, one of the major differences between these two libraries is the students at each campus.

The Simpson Library serves mainly traditional students; the Stafford Campus Library serves roughly one thousand nontraditional students who take evening classes at the university's secondary location. The nontraditional students attending the Stafford campus are diverse. They tend to be older, they have careers, and many have families. Additionally, they are all commuters who live anywhere between Washington, D.C., and Richmond, Virginia. They visit the Stafford campus only once or twice a week to attend class or work on their course assignments. Some students drive to the Stafford Campus Library to seek the assistance of the library staff, but a vast majority of them interact with the library using only the Internet or telephone.

MOTIVATION

The subject guide or pathfinder has been used as a starting point for student research at many colleges and universities. This holds true at the UMW Libraries, where subject liaisons create and maintain online subject guides for the major courses of study offered by the university. These web-based pathfinders usually consist of a subject librarian's contact information and an alphabetized collection of important print and electronic resources for a specific subject area. This design is both practical and functional, but it is also very outdated. This alphabetized list of resources is the same type of subject guide I first encountered while pursuing my library science degree in 2000. Since that time, the Internet has changed and new technologies have appeared, but the format of the UMW library subject guide has remained unchanged.

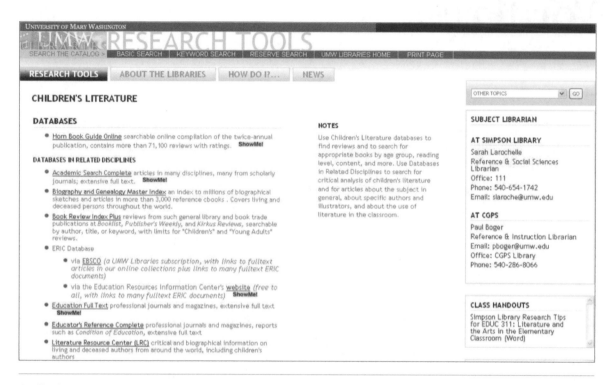

Stafford Campus Library's Subject Guide 1.0.

In the spring of 2008, I became interested in modernizing our subject guides. My motivation really grew out of my interactions with the students at the Stafford campus. Many of them expressed frustration at using the UMW Libraries website because it was too difficult to find the information they needed. The expectation was that the website and online resources would function like the commercial search engines and popular websites that students use in their daily lives. What they encountered was a cumbersome library website heavy with text, links, and library jargon such as databases, interlibrary loan, and catalogs.

UMW Libraries home page.

This inability to navigate the library website was creating the perception that it was a frustrating and time-consuming research maze that failed to produce results. The usual response was to then look outside of the library to locate needed information. Despite my warnings about the questionable quality of some Google or Wikipedia search results, students knew that information competitors like these could serve up quick and easy bites of information.

To me there was an obvious problem, and as the library liaison to the Stafford campus community, I wanted to address it. If one of the Stafford campus students said, "The library doesn't have what I need," I would respond to these statements by working with the students to prove that the library did, in fact, have what they needed. Although I was successful in leading some students back to the library's resources, I wondered how many students the library was losing. How many students failed to discover the databases or subject guides because of poor promotion and visibility?

I was convinced that the UMW Libraries needed to simplify the intimidating appearance of the website home page so that students could quickly and easily locate the tools and information needed to complete their research. After all, I felt I could spend more time focusing on information literacy if could spend less time discussing how to manage the website. Unfortunately, redesigning a library website is no small task, and it requires the energy of more than one librarian. Since a major redesign was impossible, a minor redesign, focusing on the outdated subject guides, seemed like the obvious choice by which to make a substantial change for improving the library experience of our students and faculty.

The other motivating factor to redesign our subject guides came from the fact that the Stafford Campus Library had already engaged in multiple pilot projects using popular Web 2.0 technologies like Twitter, Meebo, Shelfari, and Camtasia. These solo projects had varying degrees of success. I felt that one of the biggest obstacles to the success of these projects was the fact that they were scattered across multiple library web pages. As the UMW branch library, the Stafford Campus Library did not have access to any prime web real estate, and without acceptance for these Web 2.0 experiments at an organizational level, these projects were forced to live two or three layers below the UMW Libraries home page.

INSPIRATION: FROM LIBGUIDES TO WORDPRESS

While I searched for subject guide inspiration, Jami Bryan, the Stafford Campus Library manager at the time, suggested that I visit the LibGuides display at the Computers in Libraries Conference (2008) in Crystal City, Virginia. On her recommendation I visited the Springshare booth, and I was impressed with what I saw. Springshare's popular LibGuides service (http://springshare .com/libguides/) allowed librarians to redesign their subject guides easily by choosing from a selection of customizable templates. Tabbed pages allowed librarians to organize and present information in a fashion that made for easier discovery by library visitors, and a wonderful tagging feature provided students another means by which to locate and identify resources. Lib-Guides was also creative, with the ability to incorporate media and multiple Web 2.0 resources like Twitter, Delicious, and Facebook. LibGuides also provided a simple way to embed videos, RSS feeds, and widgets directly into a guide so that they could easily be discovered by the individuals visiting that guide. Last but not least, I thought LibGuides was visually appealing. It was a true move from Library 1.0 to Library 2.0. It was exactly what I wanted for UMW Libraries.

In the fall of 2008, Jami and I met with the university librarian to present our case for joining the LibGuides community. By that time, the national economic situation was making an impact on library budgets across the county. Faced with the possibility of budget cuts, UMW Libraries simply could not afford to join LibGuides at that time.

Although disappointed by our inability to participate in LibGuides, Jami and I were determined to make some substantial changes to our subject guides. At that time, Jami said, "If we can't buy LibGuides, we should just make our own subject guides using WordPress." I was intrigued by the possibility of moving forward with Jami's WordPress idea, but changes in library staff, a failed attempt at collaboration, and conflicts with our normal responsibilities forced us to delay implementation. As this proposed idea began to fade into obscurity, I decided to revive this experiment as a personal project during the summer of 2009.

LEARNING WORDPRESS VIA UMW BLOGS

The decision to use WordPress was based largely on the fact that it was already in heavy use at the university through the UMW Blogs program. UMW Blogs (http://UMWBlogs.org), released in 2007, quickly became the preferred publishing platform for students, faculty, and organizations across the university. In three short years, the use of WordPress via UMW Blogs grew to over 5,700 users and 4,100 blogs. In addition to being a popular and convenient web publishing option, WordPress is also an open source tool. It cost the library nothing to participate. I simply had to create an account in UMW Blogs and get to work. Once my account was created, the real learning began.

The first and obvious challenge was to teach myself how to use WordPress. I had never created a blog before, and I began to regret seriously my decision to undertake such a project when I first saw the WordPress dashboard. Posts, pages, plugins, widgets, and gravatars were all relatively foreign to me. I had read articles about using these items to create blogs, but I had never tried to do it myself. I spent hours playing with the WordPress settings and features. Every time I adjusted a setting or added a plugin, I would view the test blog to see what the effect was. After a short period of experimentation, the language, structure, and functions of WordPress began to make sense.

My greatest concern about WordPress was that it would not offer the ability to incorporate multiple Web 2.0 resources. I quickly discovered that my assumptions about WordPress were very wrong. There were so many widgets and Web 2.0 tools at my disposal that it was difficult to decide what to include on these new guides. Besides having an abundance of tools, plugins, and widgets created by the WordPress community specifically for WordPress users, many popular sites such as Twitter, Meebo, and YouTube allow you to generate your own HTML code to embed directly into a WordPress blog. Additionally, some of the major database vendors like EBSCO and Wilson allow you to create customized fedcrated search widgets. With a few clicks, I was able to create a search box that would cross-search multiple databases, and I could embed this search box directly into the sidebar of my experimental blog.

Needless to say, it was difficult to decide which tools would be valuable to students once they accessed the library subject guides. Jami and I had different opinions as to what should be included. The Stafford Campus Library was already using Meebo, Shelfari, Twitter, and video tutorials. These new blogs seemed to be a natural spot by which we could showcase these tools all in one location. I also felt our students could benefit from some creative uses of RSS feeds, so I experimented with some free RSS aggregators. WordPress does have a variety of ways to generate RSS feeds. Personally, I found these RSS options functional but very visually unappealing. I then decided to use some of the free RSS aggregators available from WidgetBox. These too were frustrating. One RSS widget would not update properly, and the other was discontinued by its creators.

My fallback solution was to create an RSS feed using Twitter. The Lists feature in Twitter allows you to create a list of your favorite publication's tweets. Twitter then provides you with the HTML code for your widget, which can then be embedded directly into WordPress. The Twitter widget was easy to create and customize, and based on my experience with other RSS aggregators, the Twitter list was technologically stable. SlideShare, the online presentation-sharing website, provided a widget that allowed for a creative way to distribute the presentations I use in my library instruction classes. I also felt commuter students might be interested in the WorldCat widgets that allow users to search for books at the UMW Libraries or other local libraries. We were also interested in using the widgets for Delicious and Zotero as a means of sharing popular websites being used in specific courses. All of these widgets were intriguing and had great potential, but "adopting every Web 2.0 tool is not the solution."[1] The wonderful flexibility of WordPress allows you to offer all sorts of information, but we had to be careful to avoid information overload. Cluttering the new subject blog with too many Web 2.0 accessories would defeat the purpose of offering a more simplified and user-friendly subject guide.

In addition to the many widgets that could be employed in a WordPress blog, WordPress also provides access to a variety of plugins that can be used to improve the functionality of a blog. Many plugins could be installed and activated with a simple click. More advanced plugins required you to add a bit of code to the CSS of the page. Although adding this extra coding sounded intimidating, it proved rather easy because instructions were readily available in the WordPress plugin directory. Of the hundreds of free plugins available through the directory, I used only a dozen. Some of the more useful plugins for creating a library subject guide were the Broken Link Checker, a Creative Commons License, and a poll-generating feature, but by far the two most useful and vital tools I had access to through UMW Blogs were the Akismet spam filter and Google Analytics. Akismet was already active for any blog that was created through the UMW Blogs network, and Google Analytics could be activated in a few simple steps.

DESIGN AND APPEARANCE

The ultimate appearance of our blog was determined by the templates available through UMW Blogs. Though a variety of templates were available, I was frustrated with the blog templates available to me. The inability to customize many of the templates created problems with the dimensions of the sidebars, blog colors, and the size and style of the typeface. I also discovered visual inconsistencies when the blogs were viewed in different web browsers. These display problems were difficult to overcome. When I tried to embed a new widget, I would often discover that the widget could not fit into the dimensions of the blog's sidebars. I was left with a sloppy display of widgets that spilled into the main column of the blog. For some of the widgets, I could alter the dimensions of the widget in the HTML code, but I had to abandon the more difficult widgets entirely.

Since this redesign was planned only for the Stafford Campus Library, we had to keep some level of design consistency with all the other subject guides being used at the Fredericksburg campus. This forced us to create a blog header that matched what was currently being used on the UMW Libraries website. This task was accomplished by Jami, who created a blog header that seamlessly matched the header on the UMW Libraries home page. With a little extra effort, the header was then inserted on the new subject blog so that the appearance was still very similar to the subject guides being used at the Simpson Library.

PARTICIPATION AND BUY-IN

Jami and I demonstrated our prototype at one of our library departmental meetings. Although our colleagues were complimentary of our work, we failed to generate any additional participation in our subject blog experiment. Our inability to gain additional library support was a disappointment, but it was not entirely unexpected. After all, asking librarians to essentially redo all existing guides is asking for a serious commitment of time and energy. This task would require the entire reference staff to learn WordPress, develop a standard template for multiple subject areas, decide which common features to adopt, and then repopulate these subject guides with much of the same content that already existed on the subject guides currently being used throughout the UMW Libraries. Jami and I needed to prove that this project had long-term substantial value for our users before it would be embraced throughout our library organization.

Nevertheless, we continued to move the project forward. The distinct differences between the Stafford Campus Library and the Simpson Library contributed to our ability to move ahead without the involvement of the staff at the Simpson Library. Because of a different geographic address and a different student body, the Stafford Campus Library has been able to experiment with new technologies that are quite often used only by students enrolled at the Stafford campus. This has allowed the Stafford Campus Library to function as a "technology playground" where we can freely experiment without having to gain library-wide acceptance. Any impact created by additional workload or technology training was felt only by the Stafford staff.

MARKETING

As the manager of the Stafford Campus Library, Jami wanted to have our subject blogs available by the start of the fall semester of 2009. I wanted to wait until January 2010 so that I could continue experimenting. Honestly, if Jami did not overrule my perfectionist tendencies, these blogs might still be in the development phase. So I agreed, and we targeted the fall semester as our release date.

Stafford Campus Library's Subject Guide 2.0.

With that time rapidly approaching, the Stafford library staff had to market our new guides quickly and directly. Jami publicized the blogs in a library announcements e-mail to the Stafford campus faculty. We posted announcements on Facebook, Twitter, and the Stafford Campus Library's portion of the UMW Libraries website. If a faculty member approached the reference desk with a question, we quickly segued the conversation into a discussion about the guides we developed. Finally, our last marketing attack before the semester began was to offer an open session for the Stafford campus faculty in which we could demonstrate the new subject guides that would be available to the Stafford campus community.

MAINTENANCE

Maintenance of these new blogs was a serious time commitment. Content had to be created, tags had to be assigned, and links had to be maintained. At times I would discover that a free widget was discontinued by its creator or a plugin was removed by the administrator of UMW Blogs because of technical conflicts with the WordPress system. These blogs required some extra vigilance to ensure that everything was functional and current.

The positive side of the maintenance of a WordPress blog was the WordPress community. If I had any sort of technical question about our blogs, I could easily search the WordPress Forum for assistance. The WordPress community does an excellent job of sharing information and providing assistance to other WordPress users. If I couldn't find a preexisting answer in these help forums, I could post my own questions to the forum and receive a fast, detailed, and helpful answer. It was impressive. I also benefited from the assistance provided by the campus administrator of UMW Blogs, Jim Groom. Jim Groom is the WordPress guru at UMW.

If I was struggling with a blog technicality, I could simply contact Jim and my solution was forthcoming.

CONCLUSIONS

I started this redesign with no experience in WordPress. In a couple of weeks, I taught myself to create multiple blogs, install plugins, embed widgets, and create and tag content with little effort. The result was an inexpensive and creative way to move the Stafford Campus Library's subject guides into the Web 2.0 world.

WordPress has the potential to create rich, interactive subject guides that are just as impressive and multifunctional as LibGuides; the weakness of WordPress lies in the people using WordPress. Though WordPress did a great job providing me with all the tools necessary for creating and publishing a blog, my lack of advanced web coding skills prevented me from utilizing WordPress to its fullest potential. In skilled hands WordPress can be developed into an impressive website, as demonstrated by the new WordPress-inspired UMW home page (http://www.umw.edu). Given the opportunity to collaborate with the creators of the new university website, I would have access to the technical expertise necessary to develop these subject blogs into the polished and professional resource I originally imagined.

Was it our intention to replicate LibGuides? Not at all. I consider LibGuides to be the gold standard for developing content-rich, interactive library subject guides. If the UMW Libraries budget was not an issue in 2008, we probably would have joined the LibGuides community, and Jami and I would never have embarked on this project. All of our work with these subject blogs was born of the desire to simplify and improve the library experience of our students. For us, WordPress was the obvious choice to accomplish this goal. Not only was WordPress free, but it also allowed us to incorporate many of the same tools and features that make LibGuides so fantastic.

How does WordPress compare to LibGuides as a means of creating innovative subject guides? Although I can judge WordPress and LibGuides only according to my limited experiences with this one project, my opinion is that the two options are comparable but have obvious differences. Overall, I found WordPress to be brilliant in its simplicity and versatility. In very little time any novice can create and publish a WordPress blog that provides access to many of the same features available in LibGuides. By far the most difficult and time-consuming task of using WordPress for this project was learning the technology and then designing the appearance of the new subject guide according to the templates to which I had access.

I really enjoyed the creative flexibility of WordPress, but visually I failed to create a blog that is as seamless and professional as LibGuides. My blog presentation is patchwork because of the limitations of my selected template and the use of widgets generated from multiple web sources. The Stafford campus blogs could truly benefit from a template that looks more like a website and not like a blog. There are more sophisticated WordPress templates available, but I have not had the opportunity to explore them for the purposes of UMW Libraries. Another drawback with my approach for creating these subject guides was my dependence on free widgets and plugins. I can say from experience that the companies and individuals who offer these free tools may start charging a fee for them. I am not surprised by this financial fact, but when you are developing a web resource with no financial support you are limited to tools you can afford.

UMW Libraries followed the open source solution for creating subject guides; some libraries may find the commercial solution offered by LibGuides to be a better fit for their organizations. As a tool for creating subject guides, LibGuides may be easier to learn than WordPress. I was encumbered with learning a new technology, searching for a customizable template, and designing the appearance of my new guides; LibGuides simplifies the technology learning curve by providing its customers with access to templates and Web 2.0 tools that have been formatted and tested to function smoothly within the LibGuides system. Additionally, the problems I experienced using widgets from multiple web sources is not a problem for LibGuides because its widgets and content boxes have been standardized to operate neatly within the LibGuides program as well.

Technical support is another critical issue. The WordPress Forum was an excellent resource for assistance, and the WordPress community is helpful in supporting other bloggers. End users must then apply these solutions to their own blog dilemmas. Not to be outdone, Lib-Guides also offers a community help feature via the Springshare Lounge. The biggest difference is that the commercial LibGuides provides customer service support to its clients. If you have any issue with the LibGuides product, you can simply contact Springshare's customer support line, and they will find a solution for you. By outsourcing much of the technical support, the functionality of features, design considerations, and technology training, a service like LibGuides absorbs much of the labor-intensive portion of creating new subject guides.

The sustainability of creating and maintaining new subject guides is an issue that I completely overlooked in my excitement to create these new resources. In addition to any sustainability issues posed by the technology, there are also sustainability "risks associated with the human element."[2] The long-term success of these blogs is impossible without a library team dedicated to their development and support. Currently I am the only librarian supporting this project. If I should leave UMW, these blogs would most likely be discontinued. In this regard, I most certainly favor LibGuides over WordPress, but again this is not a failure of WordPress. This is a failure to gain participation and support from my institution. By using a commercial product like LibGuides, you are guaranteed to have access to new features and improved functionality as long as you subscribe to the service. Plus, if your library is financially invested in such a service, there may be greater motivation to see your investment succeed.

Has this project been successful? I think so. Although a staffing shortage has prevented us from performing a much-needed assessment of these guides, Google Analytics does prove that our blogs receive a lot of web traffic, and informal feedback from the Stafford campus community has been positive. Still, I am skeptical about basing the assessment of a project like this on the number of web hits or the opinions of a small group of individuals who kindly share their feedback with the library. Project success should be assessed by the value it adds to the library user's experience.

When the use of Meebo was initiated at the Stafford Campus Library, someone asked if our students requested that the library begin using Meebo as a tool for communication. The answer is no. Our students did not request Meebo. Students did not ask the Stafford library to improve its subject guides, create video tutorials, or use any Web 2.0 tools. All of our technology projects have been inspired by the library staff's desire to simplify and improve the library experience by adapting to potentially useful trends happening outside of the library. The library must be responsive to these trends. Springshare recognized the need to improve library subject guides, and it responded by creating the very successful LibGuides. UMW Libraries responded to a similar need by using WordPress to create our own version of Subject Guide 2.0. Though LibGuides is definitely the leader in creating dynamic, multifunctional subject guides, our open source approach demonstrates not only the potential of WordPress in libraries but also the creativity of librarians driven by the professional desire to improve the library experience of its community.

Paul Boger has been the library manager at the University of Mary Washington's Stafford campus since 2010. Before becoming library manager, Paul served as the Stafford campus reference and instruction librarian. Before joining the University of Mary Washington, he was the reference/worldwide media services librarian at Embry-Riddle Aeronautical University. Paul holds a BA in English from St. Bonaventure University and an MLS from Indiana University. His professional interests include developing and promoting online library services for distance learning and commuter students.

NOTES

1. Sara Morris and Darcy Del Bosque. "Forgotten Resources: Subject Guides in the Era of Web 2.0." *Technical Services Quarterly* 27, no. 2 (2010): 178.

2. Brian Kelly, Paul Bevan, Richard Akerman, Jo Alcock, and Josie Fraser, "Library 2.0: Balancing the Risks and Benefits to Maximise the Dividends," *Program: Electronic Library and Information Systems* 43, no. 3 (2009): 311–327.

Creating Digital Archives with WordPress

Kelli Bogan

Kelli Bogan discusses the approaches taken by several archival institutions using WordPress, the affordances inherent in the CMS for archives, and how it may, in the future, be an even better fit for the archival community.

WordPress has become much more than a blogging tool and is now one of the most widely used open source CMSs worldwide. The expansion of Word-Press's role means that all sorts of organizations are considering this software to manage their collections; one such possibility is for archives to use this tool to display their digital content. Here we look at what CMS options are available for digital archives (sometimes more broadly referred to as digital libraries), how archives are currently utilizing WordPress, and the possibilities the release of WordPress 3.0 creates for digital archives.

CMS FOR DIGITAL ARCHIVES

Before delving into the world of WordPress, let's look at other CMSs that are available for digital archives. There are large CMSs designed without a specific audience in mind like Drupal and Joomla. Others were designed specifically for libraries, archives, and museums; these include CONTENTdm, Greenstone, and Omeka.

Drupal (http://drupal.org) is a PHP/MySQL-based, open source CMS that has been around since 2001. It was not designed specifically for libraries, archives, and museums and can be used for anything from personal blogs to corporate sites. It has a sophisticated programming interface that can be daunting to new users. Once its steep learning curve is overcome, Drupal allows extensive customization and social features, and it has a large open source community supporting it. One of the biggest downsides of Drupal is that it is considered to be more developer friendly than user or designer friendly.

Joomla (http://www.joomla.org), like Drupal, is a PHP/MySQL-based, open source CMS that was not designed specifically for libraries, archives, and museums. It has been

111

available since 2005 and is considered relatively user friendly. It is also thought to be flexible and allows for extensive customization if the user has the appropriate technological skills. Joomla's biggest disadvantage is that it cannot create multisites.

CONTENTdm (http://www.contentdm.org), distributed by OCLC, is a digital content management application designed specifically for libraries, archives, and museums that has been used widely since 2001. It runs on a Windows-based system and allows for integration with other OCLC products, including WorldCat. CONTENTdm can be hosted locally or through OCLC. It claims to handle any file type and can be used as a digital library, an institutional repository, or a combination of the two. It is an out-of-the-box system, but customization is possible through an API. It allows for batch processing and is standards-based, including Z39.50, Dublin Core, VRA, OAI-PMH, and METS. The major disadvantages of CONTENTdm are that it is a pay service, with price increasing based on number of items, and that it does not have the Web 2.0 functionality desired by many institutions.

Around since 1996, Greenstone (http://www.greenstone.org) was developed as an open-source suite of software tools by the New Zealand Digital Library project for the building and distribution of digital library collections. This software allows users to create content in a variety of formats, including JPG, MP3, and PDF, that can be published on the Internet or to a CD-ROM. It is platform independent and uses Dublin Core as its default metadata standard, although any standard can be used. The limitations of Greenstone are that it is item-centric, contains complicated URLs, and is difficult to authenticate and add users.

Another open source product designed for libraries, archives, and museums is Omeka (http://omeka.org). Developed and supported by George Mason University's Center for History and New Media, Omeka is a PHP/MySQL-based system that is Dublin Core and OAI-PMH compliant. It is a user-friendly, web-based interface that can be customized through themes and plugins. Omeka also contains a variety of Web 2.0 features, including comments and tagging, and it also has an exhibit builder that allows users to create online exhibits.

So, why should archives consider WordPress over one of these options? For one thing, as its popularity has increased, potential digital archive creators may already be using WordPress in their everyday lives, allowing them to work in a familiar and comfortable environment. WordPress is considered one of the most user-friendly programs available, with the only limitations being the user's own skills (more on that later). And, finally, there are WordPress plugins that are designed specifically for libraries, museums, and archives, making it comparable to the available specialized options. To better understand WordPress capabilities, let's look at different ways that archives can and are using WordPress to share collection information.

USING WORDPRESS.COM FOR DIGITAL ARCHIVES

WordPress.com is web-hosting software that provides unlimited database storage, automatic software upgrades, comment tracking, and use statistics. It is the "don't make me think" version of WordPress. Archives can use this version of WordPress to blog about their collections and events and to create interactive exhibits.

Two examples of archives using WordPress in this manner are the Drew Archival Library in Duxbury, Massachusetts, and the Cleveland Colby Colgate Archives at Colby-Sawyer College in New London, New Hampshire. These two archives are using the same WordPress theme, Mistylook, to create two different archival experiences.

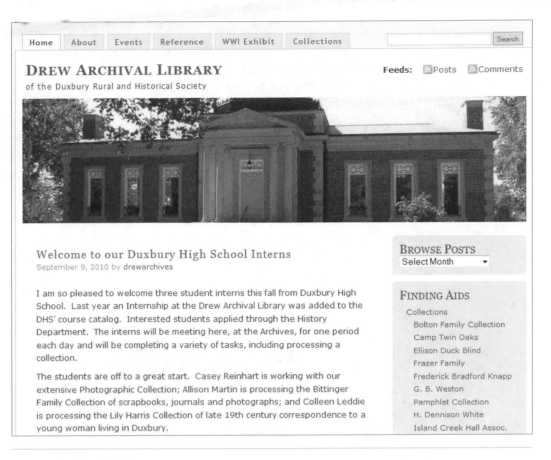

Drew Archival Library home page.

The Drew Archival Library (http://drewarchives.org) uses WordPress as both a blog to share news, events, and highlights from the collection and a catalog to provide access to the archive's finding aids. The blog feature allows the Drew Archives to use the WordPress tagging feature to identify people and subjects being discussed in a post. The archive can also place posts into specific categories like collections, news, and events to provide users with an easy way to retrieve old posts that fall under the same category.

Olive lived a long, and we hope somewhat happy life. She and Ahira had six children: Harriet, Henry, Horace, Helen, Hamilton and Harrison. She clearly liked the letter "H" (Ahira's six children by his first wife have no such naming scheme). Three of her children, unfortunately, died young. In her widowed years she lived with her son, Hamilton, who was a shoemaker. Her exact death date is uncertain, but she was still "keeping house" at the age of 83 in the 1880 US Census.

The above transcribed Dower description and the real estate deeds of the Holmes family were recently donated to the Drew Archival Library by Arthur Beane.

Posted in Collections | Tagged Ahira Wadsworth, Benjamin Holmes, Deborah Sprague, Dower rights, Duxbury, Hamilton Wadsworth, Olive Wadsworth, Rufus Holmes | Leave a Comment »

Tags and categories in a Drew Archives post.

In addition to the main page, the Drew Archival Library site includes pages that share information about the archive's facilities, allow users to ask reference questions, highlight archive events, and provide access to the archive's finding aids.

The Cleveland Colby Colgate Archives (CCCA) uses its WordPress blog for the exhibit "A Day in the Life" (http://patiencecleveland.WordPress.com), which is a part of Haystack, Colby-Sawyer College's digital archive. This exhibit focuses on Patience Cleveland, a Hollywood actress from the late 1950s through the early twenty-first century. The blog is used to post a new, transcribed entry from Cleveland's diary every day that corresponds to the current date for a "this day in history" type of exhibit. In addition to the blog posts, the site also provides monthly updates that share what has happened in the diaries thus far, Patience Cleveland's biography, and general information about Haystack and the CCCA.

A Day in the Life.

The Drew Archival Library and the "A Day in the Life" exhibit use the same system and theme to share their digital content with their users in unique ways. For example, let's compare the sidebars of these two sites. Since both sites are using the same template, each has a right sidebar. The Drew Archival Library uses its sidebar as a method of accessing its finding aids, to browse posts, and to provide users with a way to subscribe via e-mail to the blog. The CCCA uses its sidebar to link back to the college's main archive website and the digital archive, to browse previous posts and tags, and to see comments that have been made on the diary entries. These two organizations have been able to use the free version of WordPress to create sites that work for them and their users.

BROWSE POSTS
Select Month ▾

FINDING AIDS

Collections
  Bolton Family Collection
  Camp Twin Oaks
  Ellison Duck Blind
  Frazer Family
  Frederick Bradford Knapp
  G. B. Weston
  Pamphlet Collection
  H. Dennison White
  Island Creek Hall Assoc.
  J. Manville Lewis
  Peleg Sprague Papers
  Powder Point School
  Samuel and Amasa Delano
  Smith McLauthlin Collection
  William Facey Collection
  William Seymour
  Winsor Family Collection
  SMALL COLLECTIONS
    Albert M. Watson
    Alden Collections
    Annie L. Williams
    Capt. Daniel R. Glass
    Chandler Collections
    Charles M. Smith
    Duxbury Alms House
    Elizabeth Hedge Papers
    Elkanah Weston Papers
    Emma C. Paulding

COLBY-SAWYER LINKS
  Archives Home
  Haystack

ARCHIVES
  October 2010
  September 2010
  August 2010
  July 2010
  June 2010
  May 2010

SEARCH A DAY IN THE LIFE

[Search]

RECENT COMMENTS
Twoleftshoes on Sunday, September 5, 1965
Twoleftshoes on Thursday, August 26,*1965
undergroundarchivist on Thursday, August 19, 1965
TwoLeftShoes on Thursday, August 19, 1965
Twoleftshoes on Thursday, July 22, 1965

Drew Archival Library and "A Day in the Life" sidebars.

USING WORDPRESS.ORG FOR DIGITAL ARCHIVES

WordPress.org is free blogging software that a user must download and install on a web server. This version of WordPress places full responsibility on the user to deal with issues like spam, updates, and backups. WordPress.org also requires more technical skills than the .com version; CSS, HTML, PHP, MySQL, and JavaScript are all skills that are necessary. With these skills, WordPress becomes fully customizable through code and plugins. Users can create custom themes, modify layouts, and develop advanced websites not possible through WordPress.com. Archives have begun to use WordPress.org to create "catablogs."

UMarmot (http://www.library.umass.edu/spcoll/umarmot/) is an interactive catablog that was developed in 2007 at the University of Massachusetts–Amherst. The site provides overviews of the collections held in the archive, including a brief description of the collection, subject terms and categories associated with it, and links to digital resources and finding aids when available. It also includes links to the digital collections and to general information about the archives.

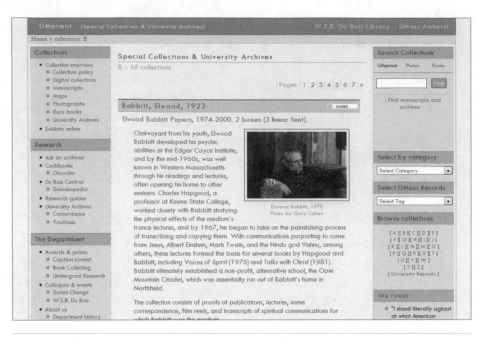

UMarmot.

The Norwich University Archives and Special Collections (NUASC) (http://library2 .norwich.edu/catablog) had a soft launch of its new catablog in March 2009. This project began as an effort to address information technology needs at NUASC, particularly the need for online finding aids. Development of this project began in June 2009. NUASC employee Laurie Thompson researched several archival management systems, including Archon, Eloquent, and Minisis 2A, but was concerned with the time-consuming workflow, potential demands for design and maintenance, and the lack of Web 2.0 capabilities in some of the programs. Thompson and the archive staff expanded their search to look at CMSs that were not specifically developed for use by archives and learned of UMass Amherst's new catablog. NUASC contacted UMass and other catablog early adopters, Drexel University (http://www .library.drexel.edu/blogs/collections/index) and the Brooklyn Historical Society (http:// brooklynhistory.org/library/wp/). After several communications, NUASC determined that a catablog was the best solution for their needs.

After deciding that a catablog was the right solution for them, NUASC looked at other blogging platforms, including Blogger and Typepad, before deciding on WordPress. Their decision to use WordPress was influenced by several factors:

- The library was already using WordPress for its library news blog, so there was already familiarity with the software.
- The other catabloggers they were in communication with were all using WordPress, and much of the advice NUASC received was specific to that CMS.
- WordPress was recommended to them over other software by Norwich's director of web communications.
- WordPress.org blogs are not remote-hosted and allow for a greater degree of control and customization.
- WordPress's support and development community seemed to be the most active and productive.

Although NUASC tried to select a theme (Suffusion, by Sayontan Sinha) that had a lot of options for enhancing appearance and functionality in the "out-of-the-box setup," they also did some theme customization. Most of the customization related to getting posts to appear in alphabetical rather than chronological order and removing the date from posts. Other customizations were done through plugins, including the print-friendly option.

The published site includes information about the archive's facilities, tools for the faculty, information for researchers, and frequently asked questions. It also allows users to browse collections by category, class year, and war. NUASC provides brief overviews of each collection, and selecting "more about collection" provides the user with a detailed finding aid, including use and access restrictions and preferred citation information.

Thus far, NUASC is pleased with its catablog and sees many benefits in using WordPress. They were able to implement the catablog with minimal support from Norwich's IT department; instead, the technology and system librarians handled all of the theme customizations and WordPress upgrades. All other aspects are handled by the archives staff. Additional advantages are that the administrative interface does not require too much technical expertise or training to start, and that they were able to get their finding aids online quickly; collection descriptions can be quickly published, edited, and illustrated directly by archive staff; they have more control over structure, content, and workflow and can match these to their budgetary and staffing constraints; they can use plugins to enhance or add functionality; the CMS offers greater potential for user interaction; and tags and categories can be used to reflect the organization and structure of their collections. The greatest disadvantage they have seen is in the weakness of WordPress's default search and the limitations of other search plugins.

At the time of publication, NUASC was focused on making descriptions of all their collections available and processing newly acquired collections. Their next goal is to begin exploring options for digitizing some of their collections, most likely starting with the university yearbooks. Although they have not reached the planning portion of this stage, they have been pleased with their experience with WordPress, and it is a possibility. Also, whatever system they eventually choose to digitize their collection, they want it to integrate into the structure of the catablog.[1]

Norwich University Archives and Special Collections.

Both of these institutions have capitalized on the user-friendliness of WordPress to make interactive sites in which to share archival information. However, neither institution is currently using it as a place to share digitized images from the collections. Transforming WordPress into a digital archive requires a little more work and technical skill.

EXPANDING WORDPRESS: SCRIBLIO

Released publicly in the fall of 2007, Scriblio (originally WPopac) is an open source plugin that adds the ability to search, browse, and create structured data in WordPress. A project of Plymouth State University and partially funded by the Andrew Mellon Foundation, Scriblio started as a plugin that allowed users to add extensibility and functionality to their online public access catalog (OPAC). However, it quickly evolved from a system with primarily display and social interaction interfaces to data created or managed elsewhere into a system that allows the creation and management of collections. Like WordPress.org, Scriblio requires the user to be familiar and comfortable with PHP, MySQL, CSS, and HTML. The installation itself is relatively straightforward, with video tutorials available on the Scriblio website that walk users through the installation and setup.[2]

The Cleveland Colby Colgate Archives at Colby-Sawyer College worked with Scriblio developer, Casey Bisson, to develop a new interface for Scriblio designed specifically for archives; the end result was one form that allows a user to manually add library or archival collections into Scriblio's metadata editor (meditor).

Scriblio meditor.

The new archival elements in the Scriblio meditor are based on unqualified Dublin Core. As can be seen from the screenshot, there is a special post form called "catalog record" that users manually complete about an item or collection. Some fields apply specifically to archives, others to libraries, and some to both. For example, both archivists and library catalogers would fill in the Title field, but the Standard Numbers field would be used only by an archive when describing a special collections book.

Scriblio meditor (detail).

Not all of the information created in the meditor is available through the public interface. Archival Source, among other fields, is hidden from users; it was created so that the digital archives' administrators can find that item again in a collection when necessary (e.g., when prints are requested or a user comes in to see an item found through the digital archive).

All public fields are searchable and browsable in the user interface. This is done through widgets called "Scriblio facets." Administrators can decide which fields should appear in the search and browse, the maximum number of results to be shown, and whether to display the results in list or cloud format.

Scriblio facets.

In addition to the meditor, Scriblio allows users to create interactive exhibits. A basic exhibit can be created through a standard WordPress page. Narrative and photographs can be added into the content box. Images can be linked, allowing users to click on an image in the narrative and go to the item record for more information about that particular item. More complex exhibits can also be created, but this requires a higher level of technical skill. To customize an exhibit, the WordPress user must create a custom template in PHP. The coding for these exhibits varies depending on the type of exhibit an archive would like to create.

There are other components that make Scriblio appealing for digital archives. It has a simplistic and easy-to-use design that is built directly on top of WordPress. The plugin includes faceted browsing and searching, making it easy for a user to narrow a search. It also has an auto-suggest search box that offers search terms based on the subjects and keywords entered into the meditor. Scriblio contains many Web 2.0 features desired in digital archives, including comments, tags, RSS feeds, and the ability to share images by e-mail, Facebook, Delicious, and other social networking systems. Finally, it allows users to track statistics through BStat (an additional plugin developed in conjunction with Scriblio) and Google Analytics.

---

berlin (Find)

Search for "berlin"
Location Berlin
Subject Berlin
Collection Berlin High Selections, November 2006
Department Berlin Winter Carnival
Subject Berlin Winter Carnival
Subject Berlin Old Home Week
Subject Berlin, NH
Collection begins with "berlin"
Department begins with "berlin"
Subject begins with "berlin"
Location begins with "berlin"

Auto-suggest searching.

There are still some places for development in Scriblio. There is no advanced search, which is confusing to users who are not comfortable with faceted browsing and searching. When browsing, there is no option to see all the results for creator, subject, or other fields shown on the initial browse page; instead, users see only results based on the most recently uploaded images in the digital archives. This setting makes users believe there are no other subject headings, and so on, other than the ones shown on this page. Scriblio is also limited in the formats it can upload. At the moment, the meditor can handle only JPGs. If a digital archive wants to include audio or video files, it has to be done through an exhibit or a traditional post. Also, each record can have only one image attached to it. Finally, Scriblio has a small user community and support system (http://groups.google.com/group/scriblio), which is a disadvantage if users do not have a strong IT department at their institution.

DIGITAL ARCHIVES USING SCRIBLIO

Beyond Brown Paper (http://beyondbrownpaper.plymouth.edu) was the first digital archive to use Scriblio. Started in 2006, it was developed as a collaborative effort between the Spinelli Archives at Plymouth State University, the Karl Drerup Art Gallery, and the Center for Rural Partnerships. The project originated with a desire to document the history of the Brown Paper Company in Berlin, New Hampshire, and was created with the hope of receiving commentary from former employees and their descendants. Beyond Brown Paper represents a single collection from the Spinelli Archives (http://library.plymouth.edu/archives). The post entries are relatively sparse, containing a generic title, the image itself, related items, and a list of subject headings. There is no description of the item, supplied title, date, or other metadata attached to the items. This digital archive is really designed to solicit information from its users.

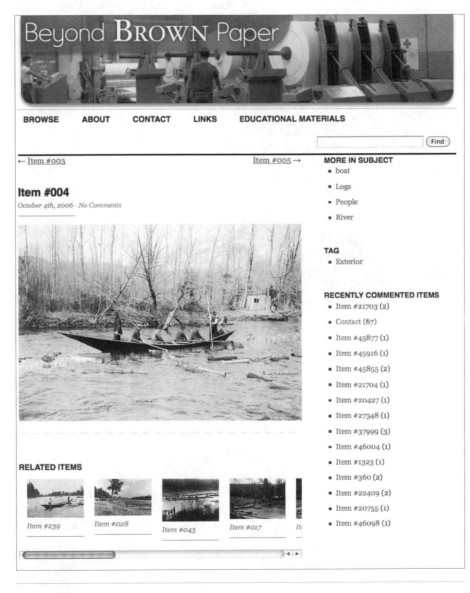

Beyond Brown Paper.

The Cleveland Colby Colgate Archives' digital archive, Haystack, was launched in November 2008, and at the time of this publication has been an active WordPress/Scriblio site for over two years. Haystack uses more features than Beyond Brown Paper, which was developed before the additional digital archive elements were added to Scriblio, and, unlike Beyond Brown Paper, Haystack is a digital archive for all digital content created at Colby-Sawyer College, not just a single collection. Materials that have been scanned and are available include photographs, diaries, correspondence, and yearbooks from a variety of collections held at the college.

Haystack.

Development of Haystack began in the spring of 2008. The Colgate Archives began researching solutions for a digital archive with some specific criteria in mind. The archive wanted an intuitive, affordable, and user-friendly interface for both the front and back end. It was also looking for a system that could be deployed quickly; handled multiple formats; had metadata built in; incorporated Web 2.0 features like comments and tagging; allowed for the creation of virtual exhibits; could move easily to a new system; and could be implemented by a small staff. The Colgate Archives looked at both pay services and open source options, including CONTENTdm, Greenstone, XTF, and Scriblio. During this process, the archive staff saw Beyond Brown Paper and liked the idea of it. However, they wanted to add some archive-specific features to the current form. As college archivist, I began a correspondence with Scriblio developer Casey Bisson, and, after this correspondence, we decided to use Scriblio for our new digital archive.

The Colgate Archives and Colby-Sawyer College did not have the IT staff to handle an open source solution, so we hired Bisson as a consultant in the summer of 2008. Bisson was responsible for installing Scriblio on the college's server and developing any customizations the archive designed. The digital archive launched in November 2008 with six hundred items.

Item entries in Haystack include a supplied title, date and creator (if known), a brief description of the item, subject headings, tags, format, transcriptions, translations, and hidden metadata including preservation information, location of the original, and physical dimensions of the item. On the public interface, users can use all of the social networking tools available through Scriblio and WordPress. They also see a list of recently commented-on items, items that other users are looking at, and other items in the digital archive that might be of interest to them based on their image selection. Users can order prints of the images directly through the website with a simple online form linked directly to the item of interest.

Another feature that Haystack capitalizes on is exhibits. Colby-Sawyer College has several exhibits that use the standard WordPress page to share a narrative with images. Examples include a time line of the college's history and an exhibit on ghost stories related to the college. The Colgate Archives has also developed custom exhibits, created through a custom template. One example is "A Needle in the Haystack," which is updated the first of every month with a new photograph.[3] A custom template was created for this exhibit using PHP. The code tells the exhibit to look for posts with an exhibit called "featured photo" and to display the most recent post with this classification.

Custom template for "A Needle in the Haystack."

To select an image for this exhibit, a Haystack administrator must go into the meditor and under Subject select the category Exhibit from the drop-down menu and describe the exhibit as "Featured Photo." The administrator then schedules the new image for the month. On the day selected, the image publishes, automatically replacing the previous one. One of the nice elements of this feature is that the "Featured Photo" tag remains with the image after its time in the exhibit, so the administrator never makes the mistake of using the same image twice.

Scheduling an image for "A Needle in the Haystack."

As mentioned above, the Colgate Archives did a great deal of customization to Haystack. Working with Casey Bisson, the archive developed several custom exhibits. It also customized its theme, basing it on the WordPress theme Amazing Grace.[4] The biggest changes to the theme were made on the home page and the browse/search pages. These pages now use a horizontal image and exhibit layout to make facets and other information more visible and usable. Also, when a user hovers over an image, a pop-up window provides a quick preview of the image and its description. This display helps users decide if they want to click on an image for more information.

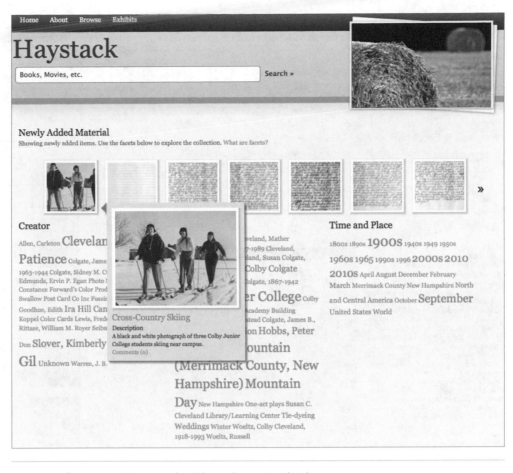

Example of horizontal layout and quick preview customizations.

Public reactions to Haystack have been generally positive, and overall the archive staff is pleased with the final product. Other archives have commented on the simplicity of the design, the ability to add comments and tags, and the faceted browsing. Users like the ability to share images easily and order prints in one step. They have no difficulty adding comments, and many Colby-Sawyer professors use the site to supplement their curriculum. Nevertheless, there are some elements that users don't like or feel could be improved. Colby-Sawyer students prefer a list of subject headings over a tag cloud (although this can be changed; without a way to see a complete list of subject headings, the list version would be even more confusing to users). The archive's older community users find faceting browsing and searching confusing. All users have expressed a need for a print-friendly option and the ability to see more than seven results per page, and they don't like the quick preview. Based on user feedback, the archive is currently maintaining two versions of the "A Day in the Life" exhibit, one through Scriblio and the other through WordPress.com. Interestingly, many users have stated a preference for the WordPress.com version of the exhibit.

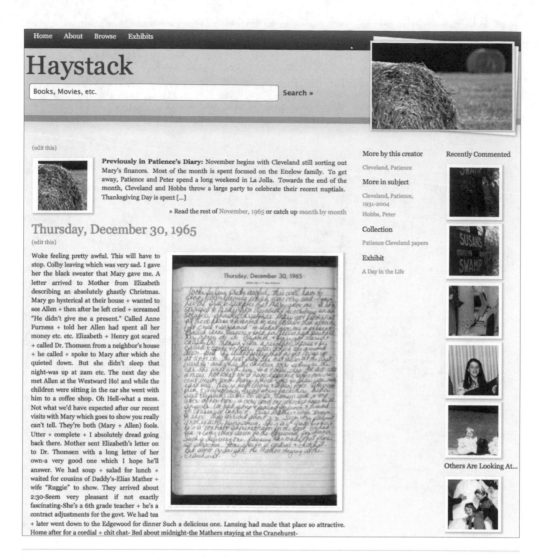

Haystack version of "A Day in the Life."

From the perspective of the archive staff, Scriblio has a simple back-end interface, and it is easy to train work-study students and other employees to use the system. One work-study student who had used Scriblio but not WordPress recently started her own WordPress blog and was shocked at how identical the two interfaces were. The exhibits are easy to create and comments come right to staff e-mail in-boxes, ready to be moderated. There is a decent level of spam that comes into the system, but the majority of it is caught by the Akismet spam plugin.

The archive has also had some problems with Scriblio. Frequently, uploading an image causes the web browser to crash, slowing down production; diagnostics have shown that this does not appear to be a problem on Colby-Sawyer's end. The lack of an advanced search as an alternative to facets is also an issue. Specific to the institution, the lack of on-site developers means that the archive has to rely on a consultant for upgrades and customizations, which is an added expense, difficult for a smaller institution to maintain. Finally, there is not a lot of support on the Scriblio website, and the forum is not very active.

THE FUTURE OF WORDPRESS

In the summer of 2010, WordPress released WordPress 3.0, nicknamed Thelonious. In this upgrade, there are two features in particular that really stand out as pivotal for the development of digital archives using WordPress: custom taxonomies and custom post types.

A post is one of five default types in WordPress; the others are page, attachment, revision, and nav menus. Basically, when a back-end user selects one of these types, he or she goes to a form designed specifically for that type. So the page form is different from the post form.

Default post form.

Standard page form.

Although these two forms look similar, there is different information attached to each form that tells WordPress what structure to give it and how to display it. A custom post type lets users create a form that works exactly for their needs; it has only the fields that the users want and create. This development is similar to Scriblio's "catalog" type—the big difference being that now it is integrated rather than a plugin. Users still need to be familiar with PHP and MySQL to use this feature through the function register_post_type. This customization allows the type to be searchable on the site, gives items in it custom URLs, and allows metaboxes to be created.[5] Tech-savvy users can now do a lot of what was part of Scriblio on their own. Once developed, it will be a friendlier user experience; users will not have to use a form developed for both archives and libraries but can use fields applicable only to their field and institution. Users could also take it a step further, making different post types based on format—such as one form for photographs, another for documents. This addition really moves WordPress beyond blogging software to a real CMS.

The other new feature that is relevant to digital archives is the custom taxonomies. Taxonomies are tags and categories that are attached to posts. Custom taxonomies allow users to create categories (e.g., subject, creator) that the user can search. This customization also requires some code in the theme's function.php file.[6] Custom taxonomies appear to be a step toward the faceted browsing and searching available in Scriblio, although it is not there yet.

Casey Bisson offered this statement on the Scriblio Google group in response to the release of WordPress 3.0:

> Interestingly, the features that Scriblio adds to the WordPress ecosystem are increasingly being done within the WordPress core. Improved support for custom taxonomies and the custom post types recently added make it very easy to use WP to manage and serve non-blog content including bibliographic records. Given that, the Scriblio features that support the display, creation, and editing of bibliographic records should be refactored to use the in-built features.[7]

Another significant feature that Scriblio adds to WordPress is the ability to search and browse that content with facets. Here again, the improved support for custom taxonomies in the WordPress core seems to be paving the way to adding the faceted search and browse features to the core as well. I am pushing for that incrementally, most recently with a patch that fixes an inefficiency in WordPress's custom taxonomy queries. That fix won't deliver all the search/browse features that Scriblio adds, but it's a start. Building the taxonomy query features into the core will encourage more development and optimization of them and externalize a significant portion of Scriblio's maintenance.

So the big question is how to refactor bibliographic records into a custom post type. Anybody want to pitch in?

Kelli Bogan is the college archivist at Colby-Sawyer College in New London, New Hampshire, where she is responsible for a full range of archival activities, centering on digital projects and outreach. Bogan holds an MA in English from Boston College and an MS in library science with a concentration in archive management from Simmons College, Boston.

NOTES

1. A big thanks to Gail Weise and the staff at the Norwich University Archives and Special Collections for corresponding with me and sharing their experience on the development of their catablog.

2. Get Scriblio from WordPress.org at http://wordpress.org/extend/plugins/scriblio/. For the Scriblio installation walk-through, see http://about.scriblio.net/download/.

3. "Colby-Sawyer College Timeline," http://archives.colby-sawyer.edu/exhibits/colby-sawyer-college-timeline/. "Haunted Colby-Sawyer," http://archives.colby-sawyer.edu/exhibits/haunted-colby-sawyer/. "A Needle in the Haystack," http://archives.colby-sawyer.edu/exhibits/featured-photo/.

4. Obtain Amazing Grace from *Vladimir's Blog*, http://www.prelovac.com/vladimir/wordpress-themes/amazing-grace.

5. For more information on the custom post type and details on how to use it, visit http://kovshenin.com/archives/custom-post-types-in-wordpress-3-0/.

6. For more information on custom taxonomies, visit http://www.1stwebdesigner.com/wordpress/essential-guide-wordpress-custom-taxonomies/.

7. Scriblio.net, http://groups.google.com/group/scriblio/browse_thread/thread/d3b0d1dc86954635.

Ten Ways WordPress Can Improve Website User Experience

Aaron Schmidt and Amanda Etches-Johnson

User experience gurus Aaron Schmidt and Amanda Etches-Johnson talk about ten simple ways to improve working with WordPress.

You are concerned about the user experience of your WordPress site. That's good. We think you should be. Although you can't create a good online experience by just sprinkling some magic "UX" dust on your site (if only it were that easy), the good news is that there are features and functions baked right into WordPress that you can take advantage of to enhance the user experience of your site—and maybe even delight your users along the way.

1. VISUAL DESIGN

If you have searched Google for WordPress themes, then you already know that there are literally millions of free theme options (*caveat emptor:* when you download a free theme, you are also downloading the theme designer's coding quirks. Your theme might work just fine for you, but if it doesn't, you might have to dig into the theme files and clean things up on your own). Choice is good, and even if your site has specific branding needs, you can probably find a theme that works for you, with a little tweaking. One of the best things about the WordPress user experience is that, regardless of your theme, there are a few design and layout cues that your users might be familiar with and expect to function in a certain way. Things like sidebars, menus, categories, and post permalinks are common to most WordPress sites, so if your users have seen or used a WordPress site before, they will experience a kind familiarity when navigating your site (which can only be a good thing).

2. CONTENT

One of the best things about database-driven CMSs (like WordPress) is the separation of content and design. Once you have decided on and tweaked your WordPress theme to your liking, the only thing you need to focus on is content. Content is important because you can't provide a good user experience with a pleasing design alone. Thanks to WordPress's simple post form, adding content is a breeze, and the built-in ability to publish posts in the future means your users never have to suffer through stale content.

3. VOICE

Talk to any web content strategist and one of the things they will harp on is authenticity, especially when it comes to social media. Because WordPress makes it so easy to distribute the content generation workflow and allow many authors to contribute, you are already well on your way to good, authentic content if you incorporate multiple authors and voices. You are well advised to include a set of content guidelines so your users aren't baffled by inconsistency in voice (not a good user experience), but be sure to allow your content folks the latitude to be themselves. There is nothing authentic about marketing copy (especially on a blog), so don't miss the opportunity to really connect with your users through thoughtful, engaging voices.

4. ORGANIZATION

Speaking of consistency, WordPress's built-in archiving is easily one of the best features of the software. Spend some time considering what sort of content will go on your blog and what retrieval mechanisms would be useful to your audience. If you are using the blog for newsy articles, date and category archives make sense. If, on the other hand, you are using the blog functionality to generate subject guides for your site, you can probably dispense with the date archives and put your efforts into building a useful taxonomy out of the category feature. Let your content drive your decisions here, and your users will be the beneficiaries.

5. BUILT-IN SEARCH

There is a usability theory out there that says that users search a site only when they can't figure out how the navigation works or when they lose the "scent" of what they are looking for. That may be true, but in the strictest human-computer interaction sense there is a whole subset of users who would rather just search your site to start with instead of using the navigation options you provide (blame Google). Luckily for you, WordPress comes with a built-in search feature that works remarkably well and includes useful wayfinding features like including your search terms at the top of the search results page (a tiny detail that pays dividends in orienting your users to where they are on your site).

6. HUMAN URLS

This may seem like we're picking nits, but having an intelligible URL scheme for your website is a smart move. For example, why make patrons look at something confusing like http://ml.lib.state.us/ys/kbks.html when your URLs could be much more user friendly, like this: http://libraryname.org/kids/books.

Sane URLs provide context, reflecting what's on the page; are easier for patrons and librarians to remember; and are more effective when used in promotional materials. With WordPress, making your URLs pretty is straightforward. You have to edit or create a special file called .htaccess, but don't fret. The WordPress Codex has a step-by-step guide to creating more effective URLs.[1]

7. COMMENTS

Simply opening up your site to comments does not turn your site into an online community. Engaging in meaningful dialog via websites takes effort. Luckily, WordPress gives you straightforward, granular control over receiving feedback from your readers without much effort. You can devote the time you save to writing meaningful replies to the comments you receive.

8. INFORMATION ARCHITECTURE

Your well-crafted content should be easy for people to navigate through and find. Although WordPress doesn't help you with the important task of labeling your pages (try card sorting for that), it does have an easy-to-implement parent and child page structure that can guide you to creating effective architecture. To layer on some more findability, take a look at adding in some breadcrumbs.[2]

9. RSS

WordPress can be extended to be much more than a simple blog. Still, built into the core of WordPress is RSS. Having RSS feeds available not only provides you the opportunity to repurpose your content in places like Facebook and Twitter but also lets those who are interested receive your library info in feed readers. WordPress has feeds for everything from posts, comments, and search results to categories, tags, and even author-specific posts.[3]

10. NO-EFFORT MOBILE

The developing trend in web design first for mobile devices is an interesting one, especially as mobile browsing becomes more capable and mainstream. Have you checked your website analytics for an idea of how many people are accessing your website using mobile devices? You should.

Many WordPress themes display well on mobile devices. The code is usually relatively clean, so mobile browsers have an easy time rendering the pages. Should you want to provide a dedicated interface for your mobile patrons, explore some of the WordPress plugins available to do just that. Most of these plugins allow your site to detect mobile browsers and accordingly serve up an appropriate style sheet. Two popular plugins are WordPress Mobile Edition and WordPress Mobile Pack.[4]

Amanda Etches-Johnson is head of discovery and access at the University of Guelph Library. She is also half of INFLUX, a user experience consultancy, and an adjunct member of the Faculty of Information and Media Studies, University of Western Ontario, Canada. She tweets @etches and blogs intermittently at http://blogwithouta library.net. Aaron Schmidt is a principal at INFLUX. He maintains a library design shop and blog at http://www.walkingpaper.org.

NOTES

1. Learn to create better URLs at http://codex.wordpress.org/Using_Permalinks/.
2. Breadcrumb NavXT adds breadcrumb navigation showing the visitor's path to the current location: http://wordpress.org/extend/plugins/breadcrumb-navxt/.
3. Learn to take advantage of RSS feeds at http://codex.wordpress.org/WordPress_Feeds#Finding_Your_Feed_URL/.
4. WordPress Mobile Edition, http://wordpress.org/extend/plugins/wordpress-mobile-edition/installation/. WordPress Mobile Pack, http://wordpress.org/extend/plugins/wordpress-mobile-pack/.

Using WordPress to Create a Virtual School Library

Anne Robinson

Anne Robinson walks readers through a WordPress-powered virtual library for her Leicestershire school.

Library Online (http://library-online.org.uk/) is the main website for the Michael Parker Library at the Dixie Grammar School in Market Bosworth, Leicestershire, United Kingdom, a small coeducational selective independent school dating back to Tudor times. The main building, where the library is situated, dates from 1828. I was appointed as the first professional librarian in September 2008, with the task of supporting the school in refurbishing the library. The planning for this took place during the 2008/9 academic year, with the main work starting in the summer of 2009. The Michael Parker Library was opened in October 2009.

The Michael Parker Library at the Dixie Grammar School, October 2009.

The school already had an attractive and well-designed website (http://www.dixie.org.uk/), but it was mainly for corporate use as an online prospectus and information point for parents. As an experienced school librarian (this was my sixth school post since 1982) and passionate believer in the power of technology to enhance teaching and learning, I wanted to create a web presence for the library from the outset, for the following reasons:

- I would be managing the old library for a year before the refurbishment and wanted to be able to offer some kind of improved service to the school. The library book stock was in poor condition and unable to support the curriculum adequately. I therefore needed somewhere to put subject pathfinders or lists of evaluated web links.
- I wanted to demonstrate to the school community that a professional librarian could have a real impact on the school. A library website could also be used to showcase exciting Web 2.0 sites—proving that libraries and librarians are involved in information and communications technology.
- The library website could be used to communicate ideas and plans about the refurbishment program and enlist contributions from the school.
- The website could track the refurbishment, showing images of the plans, photographs, and step-by-step progress.
- The development of library services could be clearly demonstrated to the school.
- The website could invite collaboration from staff and students and feed ideas into future library developments.
- The library website could also be used as a way of evaluating progress and demonstrating accountability to the school management team.

So, I was asking a lot from the website—it really needed to deliver on a range of levels.

Library Online.

I did have quite a lot of experience in writing and managing websites. Way back in 1998, I had taken a college course on creating websites in HTML. I had then taught myself how to use Frontpage and later on Dreamweaver so that I could create a library website, LRC Online, in my previous post and also a site for school librarians, Strongest Links. These sites were laborious to edit and update and caused me lots of issues, for I could not use FTP to update them at school, because of the filtering system in place, and had to do a lot of work from home. I was also becoming more and more interested in developing technologies and Web 2.0—such services as Twitter, RSS feeds, blogs, and wikis.

After I was appointed to my new post at the Dixie Grammar School, but before actually starting, I had a month's leave. During that time I began to look around for something that would help me create a new website. It would need these features:

- Capacity to create an exciting, modern, attractive design that would mirror the school colors and be appropriate for a wide audience: students, staff, parents, librarian colleagues
- Ease of editing and updating, since I would be working without additional library staff and would not have a lot of time to spend on the site
- Something that would not be blocked by the school filtering system.
- Ability to include widgets for Web 2.0 services
- Ability to have some degree of collaboration, feedback, or comments
- Something that would be easy for me to learn, since I wanted the site up and running as quickly as possible

I already had an idea that I would look at some kind of CMS, but having read extensively about Joomla and Drupal, for example, I decided that these might need more technical expertise than I possessed. Then I realized that I was already using Edublogs for my personal blog—I was happy with the WordPress software that powers this and felt confident that it would answer all my needs. First of all, I started a blog on the free WordPress.com site, but I quickly realized that I wanted more control over themes and so looked around for a company that would offer me a free trial with a hosted WordPress blog. I tried this out over the summer of 2008 to make sure that I could update the site easily and then paid for my first year of hosting.

My early updates of the WordPress software had to be done manually using FTP, which was a bit of a challenge. However, I wrote a detailed set of instructions so that I could remember what to do. More recently, the latest software updates have worked automatically, as have backups.

As mentioned, I actually started the site before my first day in my new job. So there was an issue I would need to sort out before the site could go live. I showed it to my headmaster quickly to check that he was happy with a library site running separate from the main school site. If he had not been, I would have taken all the school branding off the site and used it for another purpose. Thankfully, he and the management of the school were thrilled with the site and have encouraged me to continue developing it ever since. I also know that governors and parents have seen the site and given it a lot of positive feedback. Many students are also beginning to look at the site, although few are commenting—this needs to be improved.

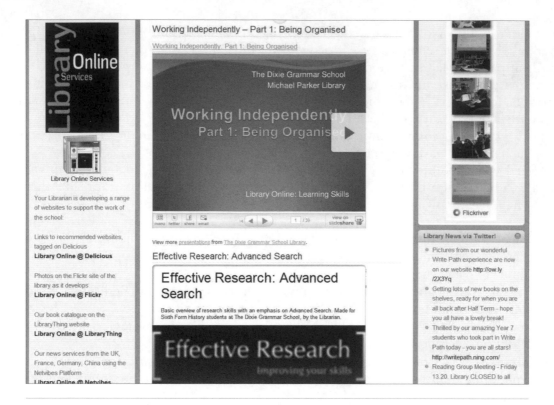

Library Online with presentations embedded on the page.

I chose WordPress, as opposed to other blogging services, for the additional reason that I could make the site look quite "unbloggy." The pages have enabled me to develop further sections to support the services of the library. For example, all presentations and documents that I use in teaching are added to the site either using SlideShare (http://www.slideshare.net) or embedded, if they are Prezis (http://prezi.com). I have also added a password-protected page to hold our new range of online resources. Widgets has enabled me to feed in many of the Web 2.0 sites I find useful:

- Links to recommended websites, tagged on Delicious[1]
- Photos on the Flickr site of the library as it develops[2]
- Our book catalogue on the LibraryThing website (we do not have a web OPAC at the moment)[3]
- Our news services from the United Kingdom, France, Germany, and China using the Netvibes platform[4]
- Presentations on SlideShare[5]
- "Reading is Fun," the wiki we use with students to promote reading development[6]
- Our video channel on YouTube[7]
- News feeding in via our library Twitter account[8]

Library Online @ Netvibes, with tab made during the U.K. general election, 2010.

I also use many more Web 2.0 services to enliven the site from time to time, such as Animoto (http://animoto.com), LiveBinders (http://livebinders.com), and Slide (http://www.slide.com). As my use of such sites has developed over time (though still in the early days), I have branded them all as Library Online Services with clear links from the main site.

Library Online with a slide embedded, also showing our Flickr widget on the right-hand side.

Now that the site has been running for two years, I am trying to plan for its development. Here are some issues I need to think through:

- As the sole editor, I need to make sure that there is fresh content on the site regularly, particularly on the blog section, which is the front page, and make time in my weekly schedule for this. I also must make sure that I have a monthly or half-term slot for checking through the static pages to make sure they all work and that their content is still current.
- I need to get the site used, viewed, and commented on by students and school staff. Therefore, the content must reflect their needs, both curricular and extracurricular, where appropriate.
- A prominent link from the official school website might help more of our school community to find the library site.
- I must also think through the implications for the site of teachers making increasing demands on me to search out evaluated web links and make subject pathfinders. Can the site hold these, or should I look for alternatives? Would the site become too unwieldy in the future?
- There is an urgent need to make sure that I have a robust backup strategy in place.
- I need to learn more about plugins; this is an area that I know little about and have avoided, because I am not confident about uploading them to the host. I am sure that I could give the site more functionality with plugins.

Over the past two years I have learned so much about new developments in web technologies; this is an exciting time to be a school librarian. These technologies allow us to do things that were undreamed of when I started out in the early eighties. We can reach out to our school communities 24/7, engaging their interest and supporting their development as teachers and learners. This is what my WordPress school library site and its sister sites enable me to achieve, through Library Online Services.

Anne M. Robinson, MA, is the librarian at the Dixie Grammar School, Market Bosworth, Leicestershire, United Kingdom. Anne was awarded the (U.K.) School Library Association's very first School Librarian of the Year Award in May 2005.

NOTES

1. Library Online @ Delicious at http://www.delicious.com/DixieLibrary/.
2. Library Online @ Flickr at http://www.flickr.com/photos/library-online/.
3. Library Online @ LibraryThing at http://www.librarything.com/catalog/dixielibrary/.
4. Library Online @ Netvibes at http://www.netvibes.com/library-online/.
5. Library Online @ SlideShare at http://www.slideshare.net/LibraryOnline/.
6. Library Online @ Wiki at http://library-online.pbworks.com.
7. Library Online @ YouTube at http://www.youtube.com/user/LibraryOnline/.
8. Library Online @ Twitter at http://twitter.com/Library_Online/.

Many Websites, One Installation
Blogging with WordPress MU at Skokie Public Library

Mick Jacobsen and Toby Greenwalt

Mick Jacobsen and Toby Greenwalt discuss theme-based WordPress blogs as parts of a public library website.

Libraries have been heeding the call to create dynamic online content for many years, from the "Library 2.0" boom of the mid-2000s to the current craze of creating digital media. In spite of this push to chase the flavor of the month, the humble blog remains a viable platform for librarians to break out of the institutional feel of their traditional sites and showcase the many distinct personalities that work there. We chose to create a separate blog for each department at Skokie Public Library, as follows:

The Answer (blogs.skokielibrary.info/answer): current events, database training, and updates from the reference desk

The Bookshelf (blogs.skokielibrary.info/bookshelf): posts on popular reading materials and readers' advisory

The Digital Media Lab (blogs.skokielibrary.info/medialab/): instructional posts about the new Digital Media Lab (some content imported via RSS using the FeedWordPress plugin)

The Explorer (blogs.skokielibrary.info/explorer): book recommendations and program information for children and parents

The Radar (blogs.skokielibrary.info/radar): technology news and information from the library

The Soapbox (blogs.skokielibrary.info/soapbox): official library announcements and responses to user comments

The Studio (blogs.skokielibrary.info/studio): news regarding music and movies at the library

WHY WORDPRESS MU

For nearly three years, Skokie Public Library has used WordPress MU to create a unique blogcentric presence for each public service department. WordPress MU (Multiple User) is a version of WordPress that allows you to run as many blogs and websites as you like from a single installation.[1] The best-known installations of WordPress MU are WordPress.com and Edublogs. With MU it is possible to have different plugins, themes, contributors, and administrators for different installations but a single login for content creators.

We decided WordPress MU was the best fit for our needs, for several reasons:

Ease of use. MU's WYSIWYG editor and user interface reduced the learning curve for those staff less familiar with web publishing software.

Unique blog spaces. Each space in the library has its own unique feel. Patrons coming in for reference or research assistance often have different needs from those looking for a movie to watch. To play to each of these audiences, we felt it was important for each area to have a distinct presence. Having separate blogs allowed us to complement the color scheme used on the rest of the library's website.

User profiles. Each blog has its own set of library staff contributing posts, but certain staff may contribute to multiple blogs. Having all blog profiles stored under one WordPress installation meant that each staff member had to keep track of only one login for all of their blog responsibilities.

Permission levels. Site administrators can dial back access to certain parts of the blogs, to make sure content contributors cannot make changes to the overall theme. This frees staff to focus on content without risk of "breaking" the site.

Once each of these blogs was set up, we used the main page (http://blogs.skokielibrary.info) as a "meta-feed" of the newest post from each blog.

WHAT DO OUR CONTENT CREATORS THINK?

One of the most important considerations when choosing a CMS or blogging platform is the content creators' (blog authors in our case) interface. The website architect needs to provide an easy way for the content creators to, well, create content.

When the Skokie Library blogs rolled out, we had a few complaints about easily fixed and occasionally overlooked issues, but all our content creators were pleased overall. The back-end interface was intuitive. Content was easy to add and edit. Tagging and selecting categories was simple. Adding and positioning images, a major bugaboo for many CMSs, was no problem. Adding videos was a snap with the Viper's Video Quicktags plugin.[2]

Many of our content creators had experience with Drupal and were shocked at how easy it was to add and edit content in WordPress in comparison. This is not meant as a shot at Drupal (I, Mick, am a huge Drupal user/fan/devotee) so much as a nod to a major strength of WordPress over all other CMSs.

CONCLUSIONS?

At this point, the increasing robustness of major CMSs like WordPress is cause for equal parts celebration and frustration. On one hand, it has never been easier for staff at all levels to create content and engage their patrons across a variety of social media. On the other, having so much variety puts us at risk of splintering our audience. With organizational and time resources at a premium, maintaining a blog as a parallel presence to the regular website may not be sustainable. Although having separate presences for each blog had some success at the beginning, the continued fragmentation of library web presences makes it difficult for staff to focus on just one site. This puts the overall flow of content at risk.

Does that mean we should scrap the blogs? Hardly. The flexibility offered by the modern CMS means that our websites are far more likely to become more like blogs or social media portals than the opposite. Discrete blog sites can be reintegrated, using categories to maintain distinctions between topics such as research, leisure reading, and technology. As new domains emerge alongside current heavy hitters like Facebook and Twitter, subsequent iterations of the library website must be able to insert their content into all new data streams. Blog posts will continue to be the primary building block for this content.

Mikael "Mick" Jacobsen is the supervisor of adult computer labs and reference librarian at Skokie (Illinois) Public Library. He has been using Drupal and WordPress since way before they were cool and is a contributing blogger at www.tametheweb.com and tweets @mickjacobsen. He can be contacted at mjacobsen@skokielibrary.info. Toby Greenwalt is the virtual services coordinator at Skokie (Illinois) Public Library, where he works to make the Internet more human. He blogs rarely at www.theanalogdivide.com and tweets all too frequently @theanalogdivide.

NOTES

1. With the release of WordPress 3.0 in June 2010, the capabilities of WordPress MU are now included as an option in a standard WordPress installation, known as WordPress MultiSite.
2. Get Viper's Video Quicktags plugin at http://www.viper007bond.com/wordpress-plugins/vipers-video-quicktags/.

Kansas Libraries on the Web

Liz Rea

Liz Rea details a statewide program to build and host WordPress-powered library websites.

Sometimes in life there are moments that seem as though the final outcome has been ordained in the stars. In Kansas, that moment came with the rise of WordPress as a blogging/CMS platform in 2006 (with version 2.0/2.5). Couple this with the fact that many of our libraries had websites that hadn't been updated since the year 2000, and you get the conditions favorable to form a great idea: Kansas Libraries on the Web. KLOW (http://www.mykansaslibrary.org) is a joint project of the State Library of Kansas and the Northeast Kansas Library System that provides web space and a library-customized WordPress installation at no cost to Kansas libraries and library organizations. As it turns out, the story of KLOW has been both comedy and tragedy, with many lessons learned along the way.

In 2006, Brenda Hough, the Northeast Kansas Library System technology coordinator, and I were looking for a project to help Kansas libraries replace their old, out-of-date, plain HTML websites. We had a good example of a program in another state that was doing something similar: the Oregon Plinkit project (http://oregon.plinkit.org), a central web host with a standardized "platform" that libraries could use to create their websites. The Plinkit project also provided centralized training and documentation, something we were interested in doing as well.

We spent a couple of months evaluating different platforms and realized that we didn't like the look of Plinkit sites; at the time, they had a very generic and uniform look across all of the sites. We wanted our libraries to be able to customize the look of their sites as well as easily add content. We looked at MovableType, Plinkit, Joomla, Drupal, and WordPress. MovableType didn't do enough and was a paid product. Plinkit didn't have the customization we were looking for, and Joomla and Drupal were just too hard to use (though they have since gotten much better).

At the time, WordPress was a relatively new player in the blog software market, but it did have both dynamic posts and static pages, generated RSS feeds for site content automatically, easily changed between installed themes, and was easy to install on the back end. It was also already in use by at least one library (Meadville Library, http://meadville library.org/), which professed to love it as a CMS for its web presence. It had a few limitations: installing custom themes on that initial WordPress version 2.0 was not easy; installing themes required FTP access, which we were trying to avoid. Editing the sidebars involved minimally editing HTML, and there weren't many themes that were customizable through the WordPress graphical user interface (GUI), though we did include a couple of GUI customizable themes in the final package. Our goal was to come up with a solution that allowed libraries to lose the shackles of FTP and the need to write any HTML at all, instead using the CMS GUI to handle all of these tasks. WordPress gave us these things, even though at first the interface was a little clunky. These limitations aside, we decided to give WordPress a go with a pilot group of seven libraries.

We spent about a month creating the KLOW "WordPress Package," which included a set of about twenty preselected and installed themes, preconfigured users, and a set of plugins to do various things such as event calendaring (EventCalendar) and e-mail lists to notify interested library members that there was a new post on the website (Subscribe2). Initially, each site had to be set up one at a time, and it took approximately fifteen minutes to bring one up on the server. We set up our first seven sites and scheduled our first full-day training for the pilot libraries, intending to do at least two full-day trainings before we thought people would feel comfortable with their new sites. The pilot libraries had only one major complaint: the sidebars were not easy to customize. Fortunately, not three months later the WordPress widget engine was built, the sidebars became infinitely easier to manipulate, and we rolled this functionality into the KLOW package.

As it turned out, the librarians had almost no trouble understanding how to use WordPress after only one day of training. All seven libraries had posted their first content on their sites and chosen a theme after that first day, and a second full day of training was deemed unnecessary. It was after this that we decided to roll the project out to the rest of the state, funded by the State Library of Kansas. A server was procured and deployed running Red Hat Linux and a standard Apache/MySQL/PHP stack. The server was hosted at a local data center, five minutes from the Northeast Kansas Library System office. The site installation process was scripted, and a site could now be deployed in just over three minutes. Sign-up forms were posted on the project website, along with helpful documentation and links. Over the next four years we had 170 libraries sign up. Training for the statewide project involved a one-day training course for the trainers from the other six Kansas library systems, who would in turn pass the training on to their participating librarians.

Upgrading the sites, in those first couple of years, proved to be a challenge. At the time, WordPress had to be updated by replacing the core files either through FTP or at the command line, which meant, since we didn't allow our users to FTP to the server, that it had to be done centrally by the administrator. Fortunately, there were not all too many updates to WordPress in 2007. We did a mass update to WordPress 2.6 in late 2007, which took about three days to complete. Each site had to be done individually.

Things went along fairly smoothly until there was a major vulnerability in WordPress that caused every site on the system to be affected. This happened at the end of 2009, prompting us to move the entire system away from the hosted physical server we had been using and toward an Amazon AWS-hosted server running Debian and the standard Apache/MySQL /PHP stack. After a few fits and starts, and a week of frantic eighteen-hour days, the service was back on the new server, with every site updated to WordPress 3.0, new themes, updated plugins, and many new back-end automation scripts enabled. We kept our site owners apprised of the status of their sites mostly through e-mail, our website, Twitter, and Facebook.

KLOW these days is mostly in maintenance mode: there aren't that many libraries left in Kansas that need websites. We have learned a lot about teaching people about websites, and a lot about what a good library website looks like. Upgrades are much easier now, thanks to the built-in ability of WordPress to update automatically from within the web interface. Our biggest challenge now is simply getting people to use the tools we have given them.

Liz Rea is the network administrator for the Northeast Kansas Library System, the 87th patch committer to the Koha Open Source ILS, and an avid user of communications technology and the Internet.

Resources

Kyle and Polly's Delicious Bookmarks

Every site we perused while writing this book, every plugin we tested, every theme we admired were all bookmarked to help us keep track of our research and organize our topics. There was a lot to cover on WordPress, and we just scratched the surface in this publication. For even more resources we left out, consider taking a look at our Delicious accounts, where we bookmarked more than five hundred sites and created more than two hundred tags combined:

Kyle's Delicious Bookmarks, "thecorkboard," http://www.delicious.com/thecorkboard/wpltr

Polly's Delicious Bookmarks, "grdnldy," http://www.delicious.com/grdnldy/wpltr

Official WordPress Resources

WordPress Resources are links to sites or pages written by the community at WordPress.org and are within the Codex, the official technical guide to WordPress.

"Backups," http://codex.wordpress.org/WordPress_Backups
Backing up your WordPress installation is critical not because of consistent threats—overall, WordPress is a stable platform—but as good practice against Murphy's Law and accidental mishaps. The Codex walks you through the manual process of backing up your database.

"Hardening WordPress," http://codex.wordpress.org/Hardening_WordPress
The WordPress Codex uses these three themes to talk about how WordPress can be "hardened," or secured: limiting access, containment, and knowledge.

"Troubleshooting," http://codex.wordpress.org/Troubleshooting

For all your troubleshooting concerns, consider visiting the Codex's "Troubleshooting" page first and foremost. As you become a part of the WordPress community you will find that other WordPress users suggest this page on forum topics before delving into full-blown answers.

"Updating WordPress," http://codex.wordpress.org/Upgrading_WordPress

Updating WordPress is extremely simple using the built-in core, plugin, and theme updater. It unobtrusively notifies you when updates are available and works speedily when in action. And though most updates are painless—even large core updates—it is important to practice the steps toward safety covered on this page of the Codex.

"Versions," http://codex.wordpress.org/WordPress_Versions

As we hint throughout this book, WordPress 3.0 was a version that received many advanced upgrades and increased functionality. But as new versions are released, you need to get up to date with the various additions and edits.

"WordPress Feeds," http://codex.wordpress.org/WordPress_Feeds

WordPress comes packed with all types of RSS feeds for your content. The system makes them a bit difficult at times to find, but this resource helps you identify the wide variety of them at your disposal.

"WordPress for Beginners," http://codex.wordpress.org/Getting_Started_with_
WordPress#WordPress_for_Beginners

The Codex has its own section on getting up to speed quickly with its own beginner guides. Take a quick look through some of these sections to help you officially get acquainted with the software.

Bloggers

The WordPress community is full of individual bloggers who share their expertise and experiences of working with WordPress. Some bloggers in this list are core contributors to WordPress and have firsthand knowledge on the technical details of the software and what's on the developmental horizon.

Chris Coyier and Jeff Starr, *Digging into WordPress*, http://digwp.com

Paul Gibbs, *Bring Your Own Terms of Service*, http://byotos.com

John James Jacoby, *JJJ*, http://johnjamesjacoby.wordpress.com

Mark Jaquith, *Mark Jaquith*, http://markjaquith.com

Chris Pearson, *Pearsonified*, http://www.pearsonified.com

Andrea Rennick, *WordPress Must Use Tutorials*, http://wpmututorials.com

Nathan Rice, *Nathan Rice*, http://www.nathanrice.net

Justin Tadlock, *Life, Blogging & WordPress*, http://justintadlock.com

Lorelle VanFossen, *Lorelle on WordPress*, http://lorelle.wordpress.com

Polly-Alida Farrington, *WordPress Tips and Tricks*, http://www.scoop.it/t/wordpress-tips-and
-tricks/

Books

Several texts among the many out there proved helpful as we wrote this book and can help you grasp some of the more difficult technical concepts of WordPress. Not all WordPress books are created equal, but these are equally great.

Technical Books

Brazell, Aaron. *WordPress Bible*. 2nd ed. Wiley, 2011. ISBN: 978-0470937815

Hedengren, Thord Daniel. *Smashing WordPress: Beyond the Blog*. 3rd ed. Wiley, 2012. ISBN: 978-1119942719

Stern, Hal, David Damstra, and Brad Williams. *Professional WordPress: Design and Development*. Wiley, 2010. ISBN: 978-0470560549

User Guides

Coyier, Chris, and Jeff Starr. *Digging into WordPress*. Self-published, latest update 2012. URL: http://digwp.com/book/

Leary, Stephanie. *Beginning WordPress 3: Make Great Websites the Easy Way*. Apress, 2010. ISBN: 978-1430228950

Community Sites

Like the individual bloggers, there are several sites where WordPress aficionados and beginners alike gather to talk WordPress. Explore their communities and vast resources to answer your questions and find your own WordPress community of preference.

CodePoet, http://codepoet.com/
Automattic's resource site includes information to help you expand your WordPress skills and know-how.

Facebook Group: WordPress and Librarians, http://www.facebook.com/groups/214139591937761/
This group formed in May 2011 to share ideas and offer support on the use of WordPress in libraries.

Facebook WordPress Group, http://www.facebook.com/WordPress/
The official WordPress page on Facebook. This is a page for news updates only. Members can comment on official posts but can't start discussions.

WordPress Jobs, http://jobs.wordpress.net
Need someone to do some custom coding? To whip up the plugin you are dreaming of? Post your job needs here.

WordPress.com Support, http://en.support.wordpress.com
Using WordPress.com? Start here with answers to lots of common questions. Includes links to the support forums.

WordPress.org Support Forums, http://wordpress.org/support/
The main support forum for self-hosted WordPress sites. Lots of discussion of plugins and themes. With nearly 500,000 topics, this can be a daunting place to navigate. Use the search feature.

WordPress Tavern, http://www.wptavern.com/forum/
WordPress Tavern plays host to over a thousand active members and two thousand-plus threads. It's a diverse community of plugin developers, theme creators, and WordPress users.

WPCandy, http://wpcandy.com
In 2010 this site changed hands, was invigorated, and is now a welcome addition to the WordPress community. Includes personal interviews, best-ofs, and well-written how-to posts.

WP Questions, http://wpquestions.com
A good repository of questions and answers. To ask a question, you need to offer a price you will pay for the best answer.

Mailing Lists

If you prefer to keep track of WordPress talk via e-mail, there are a few select lists available provided by Automattic. Most lists are geared toward developers of WordPress, but questions and comments of any kind are usually fielded. Check out the wp-edu mailing list for excellent discussions on the use of WordPress for educational purposes. Get direct access to the lists here: http://lists.automattic.com/mailman/listinfo/.

Popular Posts

There were some posts that we kept on returning to and others that we just think are brilliant. These posts come from a variety of resource types, sites, and people.

"Complete Guide to WordPress 3.0 Awesome New Features," http://digwp.com/2010/05/guide-new-features-wordpress-3/

"Create Your First WordPress Custom Post Types," http://thinkvitamin.com/code/create-your-first-wordpress-custom-post-type/

"Creating a WordPress Network," http://wpebooks.com/wp-content/uploads/downloads/2011/08/CreateAWordPressNetwork.pdf
Andrea Rennick, one of WordPress's most prolific and helpful community members, walks site administrators through the setup process for enabling WordPress MultiSite.

"Custom Post Types in WordPress," http://justintadlock.com/archives/2010/04/29/custom-post-types-in-wordpress

"Do Freelancers Do Best on WordPress, Drupal or Joomla?" http://mashable.com/2010/11/04/wordpress-drupal-joomla/

"How to Secure Your New WordPress Installation," http://digwp.com/2009/11/how-to-secure-your-new-wordpress-installation/
Jeff Starr of *Digging into WordPress* tackles a simple three-step process to securing WordPress during installation.

"Top Five WordPress Security Tips You Most Likely Don't Follow," http://www.wptavern.com/top-5-wordpress-security-tips-you-most-likely-dont-follow

"WordPress Custom Post Types & Pods: What's Next?" http://mondaybynoon.com/2010/05/31/wordpress-custom-post-types-pods/

Premium Plugins

There is a premium plugin market for WordPress that is absolutely extraordinary. Generally, premium plugins usually aren't costly—under and around $50—but are packed full of functionality. And nearly all premium plugins we have come across have personalized support built into the price.

CodeCanyon: WordPress Plugins, http://codecanyon.net/category/plugins/wordpress/

WP eBooks, http://wpebooks.com

WPMUdev, http://premium.wpmudev.org/wordpress-plugins/

WP Plugins, http://wpplugins.com

Premium Themes

Even if you aren't interested in premium themes, we highly suggest that you take the tour of these sites to see to what extent the masters of theme design are pushing the limits of Word-Press. It's almost like viewing fine art; the visual experience is inspiring and, sometimes, unforgettable.

Elegant Themes, http://www.elegantthemes.com

Graph Paper Press, http://graphpaperpress.com

Press75, http://www.press75.com

StudioPress, http://www.studiopress.com/themes/

Templatic, http://templatic.com

ThemeForest WordPress Themes, http://themeforest.net/category/wordpress/

Woo Themes, http://www.woothemes.com

Premium Theme Frameworks

If you are in a library camp and thinking about designing your own theme, we highly recommend considering a theme framework. These are bare-bones themes visually, but packed with functionality. It would simply be up to you to give them the color, imagery, and branding you prefer.

"Genesis Framework," http://www.studiopress.com/themes/genesis/

"Headway for WordPress," http://headwaythemes.com

"Hybrid," http://themehybrid.com/themes/hybrid/

"StartBox," http://wpstartbox.com/

"Thematic Framework," http://themeshaper.com/thematic/

"Thesis Theme Framework," http://diythemes.com

Index

You may also be interested in

GOING MOBILE
Developing Apps for Your Library
Using Basic HTML Programming
Scott La Counte

Using the HTML skills that many librarians already have along with flexible development tools, technology expert La Counte shows how creating a customized mobile app doesn't need to be expensive or require deep expertise. A straightforward, practical guide.

ISBN: 978-0-8389-1129-7
64 PAGES / 8.5" x 11"

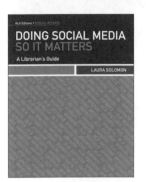

DOING SOCIAL MEDIA
SO IT MATTERS
LAURA SOLOMON
ISBN: 978-0-8389-1067-2

LIBRARIES AND
THE MOBILE WEB
CODY HANSON
ISBN: 978-0-8389-5830-8

GOOGLE THIS!
TERRY BALLARD
ISBN: 978-1-8433-4677-7

MANAGING DIGITAL
PROJECTS
IRA REVELS
ISBN: 978-0-8389-1055-9

HOPE, HYPE AND VoIP
CHAR BOOTH
ISBN: 978-0-8389-5811-7

NO SHELF REQUIRED 2
SUE POLANKA
ISBN: 978-0-8389-1145-7